S0-AAC-198

D1497334

The Best Little Cat House In Maryland

THE TRUE AND MOSTLY ACCURATE STORY OF
HOW RUDE RANCH ANIMAL RESCUE CAME TO BE

Bob and Kathy Rude

authorHOUSE®

AuthorHouse™
1663 Liberty Drive
Bloomington, IN 47403
www.authorhouse.com
Phone: 1-800-839-8640

© 2009 Bob and Kathy Rude. All rights reserved.

No part of this book may be reproduced, stored in a retrieval system, or transmitted by any means without the written permission of the author.

First published by AuthorHouse 9/16/2009

ISBN: 978-1-4490-0885-7 (e)
ISBN: 978-1-4490-0883-3 (sc)
ISBN: 978-1-4490-0884-0 (hc)

Library of Congress Control Number: 2009909334

Printed in the United States of America
Bloomington, Indiana

This book is printed on acid-free paper.

Acknowledgements

We wish to acknowledge the many people who played a significant role in our quest to help animals.

Dr. Larry Richman who taught us invaluable skills enabling us to diagnose and treat many severely ill animals.

Dr. Robert Harrison who performed thousands of surgeries for us, many of them far from routine.

Dr. Theresa Roller, Dr. James Murphy, Dr. Jantzen Strother and all the current and past staff at Belair Veterinary Hospital who provided us with medical research, support, advice and care for the animals we brought to them.

Dr. Amy Holstein who donated her services to examine and do research on behalf of the animals.

Dr. Laura Martin who examined and vaccinated the animals under our care.

Bill and Janice Steiner who provided advice on the care of animals in a sanctuary environment.

Faith Maloney and Vivian Ebbs of Best Friends Animal Society for their words of wisdom in the early years and the great example they exhibited by dedicating their lives to helping animals.

Susan Bauer for all her legal advice over the years.

Cathy Scott for the advice she offered while we were writing this book. Her experience as an author was invaluable to two fledgling authors who didn't have a clue.

We would especially like to thank Sue Ann Dilts for her patience and dedication in helping us prepare this book for publication.

We would like to thank Valerie Wilson for her help with the graphics for the book.

We would especially like to thank Bethany Swain from CNN for choosing Rude Ranch as the topic of her holiday story for 2008. Without the influx of support from that story, we may have never written this book.

Thanks to Devon Sheldon, one of our younger volunteers, for taking the photo we used on the cover of this book.

Thanks to all our employees, past and present, for dedicating their time to helping us care for the animals.

We wish we could individually thank everyone who played a role in making Rude Ranch successful in its goal to help animals. Unfortunately, that would encompass the entire book. So we collectively thank our families, adoptive families, contributors, supporters and volunteers, many of whom have followed Rude Ranch from the very beginning. Without your support, we couldn't have helped nearly as many animals.

Lastly, thanks to Ziva, the little twelve ounce, one-eyed kitten that came into our lives while writing this book. She was found in a creek bed barely clinging to life by two fellow rescuers. They brought her to us and she became the all encompassing editor that watched (and slept) over almost every word of this book.

Contents

Preface

The interview that introduced my husband Bob and me to the world was scheduled for a Saturday afternoon in December. CNN reporter Bethany Swain arrived just as the snow began to fall. Within a few minutes she had all her video equipment set up and ready to go in front of our carefully decorated Christmas tree.

As the interview progressed, I began to reflect on the history of our animal sanctuary and all the adventures that led us to this point. When it all started fifteen years ago, who would have thought two computer nerds working for the Census Bureau would end up on CNN talking about their life's work with animals? We certainly didn't. I guess you never know where one little decision will take you in life. For us it was the decision to help a colony of cats behind the family restaurant.

While Bethany asked questions about our life and our decision to start Rude Ranch, I was praying the cats wouldn't knock over the Christmas tree and take out her really expensive looking video equipment. I was also hoping I didn't have the proverbial spinach stuck in my teeth, I sounded half-way intelligent, and the camera really didn't add ten pounds. Still, every time something furry sauntered by, I worried. Fortunately, the cats cut us a break, and in an unusual show of support, behaved themselves. Maybe it was the earlier threat of Santa bringing them coal for Christmas instead of the catnip and toys they were promised.

The pages of this book lead you through our adventures in rescuing animals and how we inadvertently started an animal sanctuary. Everything in this book actually happened to the best of our recollection. Names have not been changed to protect the innocent. Any resemblance the characters in this book bear to actual people probably means those people played a role in how Rude Ranch became what it is today.

The Early Years

My name is Kathy Rude and my husband's name is Bob Rude. I grew up during the 1960's in Hebbville, a small town near Baltimore, Maryland (we don't need to be any more specific on the year). As I was an only child on a somewhat remote farm, I didn't have a lot of other kids to play with most of the time. That was probably why the animals on the farm became my best friends.

I would play with the barn cats and have a blast watching the kittens running around doing kitten things. I also had a dog named Rover that loved to go for walks and run and play around the yard. Occasionally I'd visit the pigs and cows at the barns, but they weren't all that much fun to play with.

I did the usual thing, graduated from high school, and went on to college at the University of Maryland at Baltimore County. I briefly thought about becoming a veterinarian, but remembered how I almost lost my lunch during high school biology class (never take biology as your first class after lunch). I ended up majoring in computer science instead. Maybe not as interesting, but the insides of the computer didn't gross me out as much.

I finished college, realized the "mom and dad savings and loan" was shutting down and decided I better find a job. That's when I started working at the Census Bureau. That's also where I met Bob, but I'm getting ahead of myself.

Bob also grew up during the 1960's, but in Cameron, a small town in northern Wisconsin (I'm not saying that Bob robbed the cradle, but his 1960's number was somewhat smaller than mine). There weren't a lot of people in that part of the country, but there were plenty of animals and tons of wilderness areas. They also had very cold winters and very short summers. That was one of the reasons Bob and I stayed in Maryland. I did the love, honor and cherish thing at our wedding, but drew the line at the freeze your butt off in winter wonderland.

Bob always had a love for animals. Even when we first dated, Bob would talk about his pets or the animals he rescued unlike the average guy who would talk about the women he dated or his amazing sports conquests. He had more stories about animals than anything else. I liked animals too; I just never envisioned turning my house into an animal sanctuary. Well, Bob changed all that.

The earliest rescue Bob shared with me was at the age of five when a lonely Basset Hound followed him home from kindergarten. He tried to sneak it past his parents, but didn't have much luck. His parents gave him an ultimatum. The dog could spend the night in the garage, but had to go somewhere else the next day.

That night the garbage man stopped to pick up their trash. Bob knew he had a couple of dogs at his house; so, he summoned up the courage and talked to him about the dog. After a few minutes of pleading, the garbage man agreed to take Cleopatra, the name Bob had given the Bassett Hound. Not a very formal or sophisticated process, but I guess it was Bob's first official adoption.

Bob's parents weren't big on having pets, but did give into the kids occasionally. Bob and his sisters, Linda and Diane, managed to talk them into three kittens at an early age. They also had two hamsters and two parakeets. Diane even taught one of the parakeets to help her play solitaire (the old fashioned solitaire using actual playing cards rather than the computer game popular today).

Bob was into all kinds of animals; so, when the circus came to town he was the first to volunteer to help with the animals. The circus people were letting the neighbor kids help out in exchange for free tickets. Bob's job was to walk the elephants. I'm guessing he had a little help with this activity, but he still thought it was really cool.

His next pet became the best pal he had growing up, a handsome Siberian Husky named Nick. Bob first met Nick on his father's garbage route. No, Bob's father wasn't the garbage man that adopted Cleopatra. His father, also the mayor and police chief of the village, started the garbage route when the aforementioned garbage man could no longer keep up with his schedule. One of Bob's perks for tossing trash cans around was the chance to play with all the animals along the way. His dad would talk to the customers and Bob would spend his time talking to (playing with) the animals. Nick was one of Bob's favorites.

A year or so after meeting Nick, Bob got a call from Nick's guardian. He had suffered a heart attack and could no longer properly care for Nick. He knew how much Bob loved him and was hoping Bob's parents would feel the same way.

Bob prepared for the biggest sell job of his life. He really wanted Nick and was determined to convince his parents he was ready for the responsibility. Imagine Bob's surprise when his mom immediately agreed to make Nick part of their family. Bob's mom had secretly fallen in love with Nick too (all that prep work for the heated debate wasted).

Nick had a lot of adventures with Bob and his family. One of them involved the family parakeets that constantly harassed him. Their favorite activity was to do an aerial fly-by on Nick's head. After months of this routine, Nick finally lost it and grabbed one of them in his mouth. Bob and his sisters screamed at him and were sure the little bird was a goner, but by the time they reached the little guy, he flew straight to his cage no worse for the experience. He never did buzz Nick again. Maybe old dogs couldn't learn new tricks, but apparently old parakeets could (at least if they wanted to get any older).

The next animal I recall Bob talking about was a green heron he and a friend found while walking along the Cranberry Creek near his home town. They noticed something out of the ordinary along the bank of the creek. They went to investigate and found what appeared to be a dead green heron. Then one of its eyes's blinked. Bob picked up the bird and carried it back to his parent's garage. They checked it for injuries and found it had been shot once in the chest. Something had to be done soon or the bird would die.

Bob's friend sterilized a jack knife with some matches hidden in the garage (I didn't ask why they had matches hidden in the garage) and used it to remove the bullet. Being a fan of westerns, the wound was sterilized with whiskey covertly confiscated from his parent's house. Bob claimed there was only enough whiskey for the bird, none for themselves. Then it was time to consult the *Encyclopedia Britannica*, the place kids went to get information before the internet, and find out what the bird typically ate.

While the bird was recovering, it stayed in a cage in the garage. As it grew stronger they moved it to an outside pen at the neighbor's house. One day they came out to check on the bird and it was gone. The little guy had regained enough strength to fly back to its home in the wild.

In retrospect they probably weren't following the best surgical protocols or operating in the most sanitary conditions, but back then money wasn't plentiful and their families generally couldn't afford veterinarians. They figured it was better to try something rather than let this beautiful animal perish. Bob and his friend never really knew what happened to the green heron, but they probably wondered if it was "their" green heron every time one flew overhead.

There were a lot of other rescue stories in Bob's early years, but I probably should mention that Bob did go to school and somehow managed to actually graduate from high school. He was the captain of the golf and basketball teams and was involved in a number of other school related activities. He even managed to pick a college to start the next phase of his life. He went on to a local junior college, the University of Wisconsin at Barron County and then on to the University of Wisconsin River Falls to complete his college education.

He had high hopes of becoming a veterinarian when he first entered college, but his plans were sidelined by a combination of organic chemistry on his mind and the chemistry of too many alcoholic beverages on his body. He did manage to complete a bachelor's degree in mathematics and was thrilled he survived college.

During college he started dating Erin, who would become his first wife. After college they moved to Washington, D.C. where Bob started working for the Census Bureau. He was well on his way to becoming a computer nerd.

Bob also met his first two pets as an adult shortly after moving to the Washington, D.C. area. He was sitting in the living room of his Temple Hills apartment when he saw something fall off the roof of the building next door. It looked like a cat, but he wasn't sure. He ran down the three flights of stairs fearing he would find an injured animal; instead he was greeted by a little cat that just wanted some attention. He brought her into the apartment and planned to surprise Erin when she arrived home from work. They decided to keep the little cat and named her Smokey from the movie *Smokey and the Bandit*.

As it turned out, Smokey didn't move into the apartment alone. She soon gave birth to a little kitten they named Bear, from the TV series *BJ and the Bear*.

Shortly after that, Bob and Erin were married in 1985 and bought a townhouse in Crofton, Maryland. They moved into the townhouse with their two cats and Bob's sister, Linda, who had moved to Maryland in an attempt to escape the cold of Wisconsin.

Unfortunately, or fortunately for me, Bob and Erin soon divorced and went their separate ways. Bob kept the cats and Erin got the VCR. I was pretty sure Bob felt he got the better end of the deal. I never met Erin; so, I couldn't really comment on her; I just assumed Bob needed some practice at the husband thing before meeting the right woman. At least I got a broken-in model, hopefully with all the new husband kinks worked out.

That left Bob living in the townhouse with Smokey, Bear and his sister Linda. Soon his sister Diane graduated from college, took a job near them, and moved into the townhouse with them to save money on rent. Now Bob was living in the townhouse with his two sisters, two cats and two German Shepherds they had just rescued (maybe he was starting some sort of Noah's Ark). All went well except the townhouse only had one bathroom. There just wasn't enough room for everyone. They made the big decision to buy a house together. They moved to their new house in Gambrills, Maryland over the Memorial Day weekend in 1989. Bob was thrilled; it had four bathrooms, no more waiting.

Unfortunately, their two cats, Smokey and Bear, had succumbed to feline leukemia shortly before the move. It was a fairly unknown disease at the time and the loss of the two cats really hit Bob and his sisters hard. That was probably the reason Bob had a soft spot for leukemia cats.

Shortly after moving into the house, Bob and Diane were driving home from their bowling league when they saw the car in front of them hit something. They stopped and looked around, but couldn't find anything. Then they heard some meowing down in the ditch. They started calling out and this little black and white kitten crawled up on the road. He was in pretty bad shape and needed immediate medical attention. Of course it was around midnight so that didn't leave a lot of choices.

They went to the emergency vet and learned the kitten had fractured his back and had a bunch of other problems. The vet said it would probably be best to put him to sleep, but that was not an option for Bob and Diane if there was any chance of survival. They told the vet to do what he could to stabilize him and then took the little guy home for bed rest. He was never able to walk normally, but Buddy, the name they chose for him, quickly recovered and became a big part of their family.

Of course two dogs and a cat just weren't enough for a big house like theirs. One night Diane was out driving with a friend and heard some meowing while at a stop sign. She investigated and found there was a kitten hiding in a culvert. She crawled into the culvert and found not one, but two little kittens; a little calico they named Callie and a little black and white one they named Blackie. They put the kittens in Bob's bedroom until they had time to work with them and get them accustomed to humans. The kittens were a little frightened, but seemed thankful for the food and shelter.

The next day Bob came home from work and couldn't find Callie or Blackie anywhere. He searched and searched the room but couldn't figure out where they were hiding or how they could have escaped the room. When all else failed, he sat down in his recliner to watch TV. As he was settling into the recliner, he felt something pushing up on his butt. The mystery of the missing kittens was solved.

Shortly after the kittens moved in, Linda moved out; not because she didn't like the kittens, but because she met her soon to be husband, Bill. Then Bob's parents retired and moved in with him and Diane. I guess Bob's entire family wanted to escape the frigid winter wonderland of Wisconsin.

By now Bob and I had known each other for several years. We first met in 1986 when I started working at the Census Bureau. At first we didn't talk much, mostly because Bob was always tucked away in his cubicle banging away on his keyboard. He was a true computer geek.

Then one day we realized we had started dating. Neither of us was quite sure when it happened, but at some point it did. We had one of those long courtships. The dating was working well so why mess with it.

Then Bob popped the question. I know, you are thinking it was the marriage proposal thing, but that came later. This was the "do you want a cat" question. I was busy working on my master's degree and wasn't sure I wanted the extra responsibilities of raising a cat. Bob felt otherwise. He found me a frightened little torti kitten at a local animal shelter. I fell for the little ball of fluff and named her Tia Maria ("Tia").

The next few years were somewhat quiet with work, school and life getting in the way of rescuing animals. Bob and I were still dating and spending most of our free time together. Then Bob popped the other question. I readily agreed to his proposal; after all, I had already spent six years training him. The wedding was pretty normal as far as weddings go, but the wedding cake was bordering on the ridiculous. My mom made wedding cakes for a living and felt she had to go all out for her only daughter. It was a three dimensional masterpiece that required enlisting my dad's carpentry skills to complete. It consisted of twenty-two individual cakes in a heart shaped pattern. Bob had to rent a Ryder truck and recruit two of the guys in the wedding party to get it from my parent's house to the reception hall. Fortunately, for Bob and his friends, it arrived in one piece or at least in the twenty-two pieces they started with.

The Wedding Cake

Now that Bob and I were married he had to figure out what to do with his pets. Bob was moving into my townhouse, and his dogs probably wouldn't adapt well to life without a yard. The cats would probably adjust, but they were also Diane's pets. The animals were already used to living together in the Gambrills house, so they decided the animals would stay with Diane and Bob's parents. Besides, Bob's mom had become best friends with Buddy, the little kitten that was hit by the car, and would probably put up a fight before letting him go.

Of course that created a dilemma for Bob; he was living in a house with only one pet. He had built a really cool fish pond in the back yard, but he didn't consider them pets. He had to remedy this situation. He convinced me I really wanted to add a kitten to our family for Christmas. I sent him out in search of the right addition to our family and he found a cute little torti kitten at a local shelter (sound familiar)? Unfortunately for Bob, she had a cute little sister in the cage with her. Bob just couldn't pick one over the other. He took a chance that I wouldn't beat him over the head with a rolling pin and adopted the sisters together. When I got home from work that evening, I was greeted by two cute, red ribbon-wearing kittens. Obviously I couldn't be upset with Bob. We named them Billie Jo and Ashley Ann ("Ashley").

Tia took a little while to warm up to the little ones. At first she thought they were either annoying little rug rats or really neat interactive toys. Then two weeks after introducing the kittens to Tia, we came home to find her curled up on the bed grooming them. We were well on our way to having a nice little family.

Birthplace of a Rescue

I guess life was getting a little too boring for us. Remember when I said the little decisions in life can lead to big changes? Well, we now began the adventures that led us down the path to starting our own animal sanctuary. In 1996, Bob's sister Linda and her husband Bill decided to start a restaurant in Crofton, Maryland. Bob's other sister Diane decided to join them and became the partner/manager of the restaurant. It was to be named Uncle Nicky's after the man who helped raise Bill. Uncle Nicky's had a brief brush with fame as the place where the "Snakehead Fish" were first discovered. It was a national craze for a brief time and David Letterman even included them on one of his top ten lists.

Shortly after starting the restaurant, Diane asked Bob and me if we would be willing to help out with the cooking and waitressing duties. We said "why not" and began learning our new responsibilities (and wondering what we were getting ourselves into). Bob's mom also started working there as a waitress and making the desserts. I don't know if they planned it that way, but it was starting to turn into a "family" restaurant.

While working at Uncle Nicky's we noticed some cats eating out of the dumpster behind the restaurant. We didn't think too much about it until some kittens appeared one day. We felt sorry for the little kittens and started calling all the local, no-kill animal shelters hoping to find one that could take them. Unfortunately, they were all full and they didn't have any other suggestions for us. When we called the more traditional shelters and animal control agencies, they said we could bring the kittens in and they would euthanize them for us. Not exactly what we had in mind. We wanted to help the kittens not kill them!

We finally decided to take matters into our own hands and try to do something to help the cats and kittens behind the restaurant. We had heard about Trap/Neuter/Release (TNR) programs, but didn't know much about them. After some research, we learned it was a simple matter of humanely trapping the cats and kittens, getting them altered and returning them to their colony. Then they could continue life as before, but without the ability to reproduce.

It seemed simple enough to us, why not give it a try? We borrowed a humane trap and had success on our first attempt. A little grey cat about four months old was in the trap. Now what do we do? We didn't really expect to catch one on our first try and hadn't put much thought into what to do if we actually caught one.

We made a quick call to our regular vet, Dr. Harrison at the Belair Veterinary Hospital, and made an appointment to have everything done for the little kitten. We really didn't know what that entailed, but we assumed Dr. Harrison would know. We picked the little girl up the next day, paid the bill, and put her in the second bedroom to recover and to keep her separate from our cats.

That's when we realized doing the entire colony this way was going to be a very expensive endeavor. We did some additional research and came across Dr. Richman at the Save A Life shelter who performed low cost spay/neuter surgeries and vaccinations. We gave him a call and arranged to start bringing our rescued cats to him for their vet work.

In the meantime, we began socializing the first cat we caught rather than put her back in the colony. Her socialization went well, but slowly. Every night we went upstairs to spend some time with the little one, but we could never find her! She would disappear in the room no matter what we did to eliminate her hiding spots. Eventually she would appear, but we never could figure out where she was hiding. Then it was time to give her a name. We always had a hard time coming up with an appropriate name for a pet, but this kitten made it easy with her constant disappearing act. We named her Ghost.

Eventually we decided to let Ghost have the run of the townhouse. We were still planning to socialize her and find her a new home, but now that she had the run of the townhouse we barely saw her. Occasionally she would stop by for food and a little attention, but then would just as quickly disappear.

Then disaster struck Bob. He had severe viral pneumonia and was down and out for a couple of weeks. He couldn't breathe all that well lying in bed, and his snoring had become unbearable, so I sent him downstairs to sleep on the couch. I really only had his best interests at heart (if I had to spend one more sleepless night listening to him snore, I couldn't be held responsible for my actions)!

It was during one of those days while he was sleeping on the couch that he woke up with something warm and fuzzy curled up on his chest. It was Ghost. She was purring and seemed to want attention. Bob started petting her and she purred louder. I guess she thought he needed some extra nurturing or else the heat from his fever felt good to her. Of course this created a new dilemma; Bob couldn't part with her after that. When I came home from work later that day, Bob informed me we had just adopted our fourth cat.

Ghost Relaxing in the Second Bedroom

Eventually Bob recovered from the pneumonia and it was time for us to get back into the trapping routine. In addition to all the other cats we had seen earlier, we now saw a mother cat with one kitten and a male cat (probably the daddy) hanging out behind the restaurant. We decided we would trap and tame the kitten, and with any luck, find it a new home. The parents would be trapped, fixed and put back in the colony. We would let the cats recover from their surgery in a garage located on the property. Sounded easy, right?

We borrowed some traps from the local SPCA and made sure Dr. Richman was available for the spaying and neutering. It was all set up; now all we had to do was catch the cats.

The kitten appeared to be about ten weeks old. She was living in the same garage where we caught Ghost, so it seemed like a good place to set the trap. We caught the kitten within two hours. By that evening, she had been spayed, tested for feline leukemia and the feline immunodeficiency virus (FIV), given her shots and was back in the garage for her recovery.

The next morning we checked on her and she came right over to us for attention. We decided to move her from the garage to our third bedroom so we could spend more time socializing her. She really seemed to like her new accommodations. I guess it was a step up from the garage. We code named her MsNoName. After all, she was just here to be tamed and then adopted out to a forever home, but she was awfully cute. The Rude Cats were a little ticked off; after all she got the yummy kitten food, while they were trying to choke down their diet cat food.

Then it was time for the bigger challenge; catch the mommy and daddy. On Sunday, we set the traps and then went to work at the restaurant (remember Bob was the cook and I was one of the waitresses). We snuck out to check the traps a few hours later and there was the mommy kitty, sitting beside one of the traps giving us the feline equivalent of the finger. On the way back to the restaurant we saw something grey running into another building, and it wasn't a squirrel. We checked a little closer; yep, three more kittens, about six weeks old. They probably belonged to the little calico we'd been feeding in that building. Guess she was really busy that spring. We finally left for the evening without any luck in our trapping efforts.

The next morning I went back to check the traps and we had a cat, but not MsNoName's mom. It was the little calico mom. Now I had a feline dilemma, should I let the momma kitty go so she could take care of her kittens or take her in to be spayed. Chances were if I let her go, we might not catch her again. But if I had her spayed, she would be away from her kittens for at least two days. The kittens were old enough to eat on their own, but not old enough to defend themselves from the local predators. Also, I had taken half a day off from work, and the vet was waiting, so someone was going to get fixed, and Bob wasn't volunteering. We got the mom fixed and put her in the garage to recover. Now we had to catch the kittens and bring them back to our townhouse.

That was easier said than done. We had to catch them soon because we didn't want to leave the young kittens out on their own for very long. Bob reset the traps and went to check them after work to see if we had any luck. We had a kitten in one of the traps!!! Now his game plan was to transfer the kitten to a carrier and reset the trap for the next kitten, easy right? To make sure he didn't lose the kitten, he got into the car and closed all the doors. Then he opened the trap so he could put it into the carrier. The kitten had other plans and promptly scrambled out of the trap, and disappeared into the dashboard of the car. Yep, it was now hiding somewhere in the bowels of the car.

Bob had no intention of starting the car until he could find the kitten. His new plan was to call me to see if I could come over and help get the kitten out from behind the dashboard. Oops, both cell phones were in my car, so he went looking for a pay phone. It turned out there weren't as many pay phones in Crofton as there used to be.

Bob finally reached me and I arrived to help. We discovered there were about eight screws and four bolts holding the dash of a Toyota MR2 together. Once we disassembled the dash, we found the kitten had lodged its head inside the blower fan of the air conditioner. As we pulled the kitten out of the disassembled dash, the kitten started spitting, clawing and biting. I managed to hold on to the little @@## and dropped it into a carrier, but not before it drove its little kitten teeth into my finger. We didn't need to spend time coming up with a name for this one, we promptly dubbed the kitten PITA, short for Pain in the A__!!!

Even after all this excitement, Bob remembered to reset the trap for the next kitten. When Bob returned the next morning, we had kitten number two in the trap. This time Bob brought a coworker along for backup. Why send one guy to do a job when two could screw it up twice as fast. This time it went a little better; Bob was only bitten twice, and we didn't have to take the car apart.

After lunch Bob went back and kitten number three was waiting in the trap, but bad news; two more kittens were outside the trap, bringing the litter's total to five. Bob felt kitten number three might be the ring leader, at least this one bit the hardest.

Bob caught kittens number four and five later that night. By now we were smart enough to at least bring a pair of gloves with us. We put PITA and his siblings in our second bedroom until we could figure out what to do with them. We even set up a fancy kitten condo from two PC boxes we had stored in the garage. The five kittens weren't exactly happy, but at least they were safe and warm.

The next day we were racked with guilt about separating the mother cat from her little ones. She was going to have no idea what had happened to her kittens. The kittens seemed to miss their mom too. They even started nursing on each other. We made the executive decision to retrap the mom and reunite the family.

We went back to the garage, set the trap and waited for Momma Kitty to fall for the bait. Fortunately, she liked the roasted chicken enough to let her guard down. Let's just say she was more than a little ticked off when she sprung the trap; more like death to the human race ticked off.

Then we brought her home to reunite her with the kittens. We put Momma Kitty in the second bedroom, opened the trap door and hoped for a happy reunion. The kittens couldn't figure out if it was their mom or some other cat, all they saw was her backside while she kept staring at us with a "die evil human, pond scum" look in her eyes. We left them alone and came back a little later to what we had planned all along: Momma Kitty and her family were all snuggled in the box with the kittens nursing away on her. We said good night to our guests and went to bed.

First thing in the morning we quietly went to the second bedroom not sure what to expect. We had a wild mother cat and her five wild offspring living in the room. When we opened the door, things weren't all that bad. Momma Kitty was glaring at us from behind the printer with two of her kittens huddled next to her. Two of the other kittens were peeking at us from the other side of the printer, and the last kitten was peeking up at us from under the desk. For the most part, the room was intact. They did manage to knock a few of Bob's country music CDs off the desk, but that didn't bother me all that much. I guess Momma Kitty wasn't a fan of Garth Brooks or Shania Twain either. Bob loved country music, but I was more of a classic rock person. Maybe Momma Kitty and I would get along better than I thought.

So in summary:

We now had eleven cats hanging out at our townhouse. Some of the guys Bob worked with had started telling people their boss ran a "cat house" on the side.

Tia, Billie Jo, Ashley and Ghost were ready to hang a "better help wanted" sign on the door. They felt the "guest" cats were getting far too much attention.

MsNoName was getting pretty friendly; she was starting to look a lot like a Maggie or a Maddie.

Momma Kitty decided not to do away with the human race in general, just Bob and me specifically.

Momma Kitty's kittens weren't sure about anything yet, just show them where the food, water and litter box were and they were good with life.

Bob and I were considering getting rabies vaccines (we thought it might be a good idea since we kept letting wild animals bite us on a regular basis), and possibly having our heads examined (you never know, there may still be a few functioning brain cells left in there).

Bob's car still worked (surprisingly) after being reassembled.

We still hadn't caught MsNoName's mom, the original cat we set out to trap.

We thought there was one more cat with kittens on the property (at least we hoped that was all we had left).

Did I mention we were still working at the Census Bureau and Uncle Nicky's too?

Anyone want to adopt a kitten?

Maggie and Friends

It was time to really focus on socializing MsNoName. Bob brought her downstairs one night so he could spend more time with her. In other words, Bob wanted to sit on the couch and watch TV while hanging out with little MsNoName. He figured it was a good time to try; I had the Rude Cats in the basement with me supervising the sacred rite of litter box changing (yes, it was a four cat job).

Bob and little MsNoName were happily watching a rerun of *Cheers* when Bob was lulled into a false sense of sleepy kitten syndrome. He loosened his grip on MsNoName, who promptly became wide-eyed and bushy-tailed, climbed up and over Bob, and behind the couch. All I heard was, "Kathy, hurry up, MsNoName escaped." I had to drop what I was doing and run up the stairs to help Bob capture the little troublemaker. I crawled under the couch to find MsNoName while Bob covered the other end of the couch to block her escape from that direction. We were hoping to capture her before the other cats discovered what was happening.

Too late, the Rude Cats had arrived on the scene. We promptly told them to stay away, which in cat talk means "I'm missing something really good over there, so I better get closer." Billie Jo was the first to venture in. She bravely stuck her nose under the couch to discover what we found so interesting. She didn't see anything, but had to let out a big growl and take a swipe at the couch just in case. Ghost was the next to venture in. She made her entry through the drawer between the couch's two recliners, but there was still no sighting of the kitten. Tia and Ashley felt the adventure wasn't worth their time and went into the kitchen for a snack. We finally tricked MsNoName out from under the couch with the help of a can of tuna fish. What cat could resist tuna fish? It was back to the third bedroom for her. I had this desire to whack Bob over the head with my rolling pin for letting the kitten loose in the first place, but managed to fight off the urge. After all, I still had a lot of work for him to do.

Even after that adventure, MsNoName was doing much better. We weren't doing as well with Momma Kitty and her kids though. We would need to work harder at socializing them if we wanted to find them new homes. We also realized we had too many kittens in one room. They would all huddle together to resist us evil humans. We thought we would make more progress if we separated the kittens and gave them more one-on-one attention. Unfortunately, with MsNoName in the third bedroom and Momma Kitty and her kids in the second bedroom, we were running out of rooms in the townhouse.

We thought it over and converted the powder room on the main floor into the kitten socialization room. We moved two of the kittens (code named Goldie and Grey) into the powder room as our first victims. It was a little tight, but how much room would two kittens need? It was amazing how far a six week old kitten could kick kitty litter up a wall. It was also amazing how kittens had a natural instinct to shred toilet paper into thousands of pieces. I was pretty sure we wouldn't forget to hide the toilet paper next time.

Once Goldie and Grey were settled into the powder room, Bob went back upstairs to check on Momma Kitty and the rest of her kids. She went truly ballistic on him. She had moved the remaining three kittens into her paw swipe range and hunkered down to do battle from behind the printer. She wanted nothing to do with us and made that point very clear when Bob ventured a little too close. At least Bob wasn't planning to use that hand for awhile.

Goldie and Grey

We finally gave in to MsNoName's desires and let her hang out with the Rude Cats. After all, the Rude Cats wanted to break into her room to get the kitten food anyway. Their initial reaction to MsNoName was entertaining. Tia (Her Royal Highness) sniffed her, and then popped MsNoName on the ears to make sure she knew who was boss. Ashley was out and out ticked off and showed her displeasure by hissing at the kitten and coughing up a huge hairball. I guess the hairball was a gift for Bob and me. Billie Jo arrived to give her opinion, but MsNoName found her to be totally fascinating. She started following her everywhere. Billie Jo finally escaped by leaping on top of the china cabinet. Then it was Ghost's turn to check out the kitten. It was hard to describe Ghost's reaction except to say that it was hilarious watching a sixteen pound full grown cat running from a two and a half pound ball of fluff. She looked even sillier when she ran into the wall trying to run away, while keeping a close eye on MsNoName. All in all, a pretty good first experience. No actual fights and no bloodshed!

Things were going pretty well on the home front, so we thought it was a good time to get back to the trapping. On our first attempt we caught the cat we thought was MsNoName's dad. At least it really looked like a male cat. If not, we had a female cat on steroids. When we called Dr. Richman to tell him we were on the way with a cat, he said there was one small problem. His office was being painted. The painters were supposed to be done, but they were running a little behind schedule. He told us if it was a male cat he could still do the surgery, but it would need to be done outside, and someone would have to assist him.

When we arrived, Dr. Richman had a surgery table ready to go out behind the shelter. There was nothing like fresh air to make surgery more enjoyable. Hopefully he wouldn't charge extra for the view. He confirmed that yes, it was a male cat. Then it was time to help neuter the cat. I "volunteered" to hold the cat while Bob kind of stood there, with his legs crossed and a pained expression on his face. I guess it was a guy thing. The surgery went well, I could now claim surgical experience on my resume, and Bob didn't pass out even once.

We were now more determined than ever to catch MsNoName's mom. To the best of our knowledge, she was the only female we hadn't lured into a trap. We were tired of being outsmarted by a little cat. We hoped the plate of roast beef we hijacked from Uncle Nicky's would do the trick. Maybe she wasn't into the roasted chicken we had been using; she was probably more of a Midwestern cat that preferred meat and potatoes.

We put a trail of roast beef up to the trap and a huge serving in the trap. Then it was back to the car to begin the long, boring process of waiting for her to appear. She finally showed up; the beef seemed to be doing the trick. She ate every piece leading up to the trap. We were starting to gain confidence. Then she arrived at the trap, turned around, and I swear she raised her paw with the middle toe extended. Then she ran off into the woods. Oh well, maybe we'd catch her next time.

It had now been five days since we let MsNoName loose in the townhouse. We hadn't witnessed any major incidents or fights. Even Ashley stopped hissing and was only giving her dirty looks. It was time to give MsNoName a real name; we officially made it Maggie Mae ("Maggie").

Little MsNoName, aka "Maggie"

Tia, Billie Jo, Ashley and Ghost took great pleasure in bouncing Maggie off the walls; she always came back for more, so I guess it didn't hurt all that much. We also noticed Maggie brought about a new partnership between the Rude Cats. Ghost and Billie Jo teamed up to get Maggie into trouble, rather than the normal partnership of Ashley and Billie Jo scheming to get Ghost into trouble. Maybe they would all get along soon.

Now that Maggie was doing well in the townhouse, it was time for Goldie and Grey to graduate from the powder room to the third bedroom. They were always curious about things and adept at getting into trouble. Grey figured stuff out first, and then showed Goldie the ropes (Grey was a girl, Goldie was a boy, so it seemed about right). We were curious to see if they would hide under the bed or continue craving our attention.

With Goldie and Grey relocated to the third bedroom, we readied the powder room for the next round of kitten socialization. We weren't sure which ones it would be, but we waited for our Kevlar gloves to arrive before making an attempt to capture them. Momma Kitty had become much more protective and wasn't willing to give up any more of her kids without a fight.

We went into kitten capture mode. I tried to distract Momma Kitty while Bob made his move on the kittens. Momma Kitty had different plans and gathered her remaining kittens around her and made it clear she had no regard for human flesh. Yep, you guessed it; at this point she could scare the crap out of a Doberman, or at least out of Bob and me. However, we got lucky; one of the kittens ran away from Momma Kitty and was trapped between the PC and the back wall. We put the carrier down in front of him and Bob scooped him into it. This was the kitten originally known as PITA (the kitten who got stuck in the car). Our original conversation with him went something like this:

"You're a pretty kitty"

"HISSSSSSS"

"Do you want some food?"

"HHHIIIISSSSSSS"

"Do you want to play?"

"HHHHHHHHIIIISSSSSS"

We had to admit it was really cute the way his little nose wrinkled up when he hissed at us. We saw that wrinkled nose a lot. So we changed his name from PITA to HISSOR.

Despite all his hissing, and tough boy bravado, Hissor spent the entire night crying for his family. Out of pity, we caught another kitten and put her in the powder room with him. Our conversation with kitten number four was very familiar:

"Do you remember your brother?"

"HISSSSS"

"Do you want some food?"

"HHIIISSSSS"

"Do you want me to leave you alone?"

"HHHHHHHIIIISSSSS!!!!!!!!"

We named her Hissetta.

If it weren't for the lack of opposable thumbs, Momma Kitty would probably have found a way to do Bob and me in by now. We weren't sure what to do with her. She was really cute, but we were getting really tired of the attitude.

We moved on to more trapping while we decided what to do with her. We really wanted to catch the last few cats in the colony before they started reproducing. We also found another building on the property that worked better for the cats' post surgery recovery. It was a smaller building, and unlike the garage we had been using, it was almost empty and we could lock the door. It seemed like the perfect set up.

We moved the litter box and the food and water dishes into the new recovery building. Bob personally donated to the trapping effort by dropping two whole chickens on the floor of the restaurant: at least we had plenty of bait. Then we set the trap for the cat that was hanging out behind the restaurant and went home for the evening.

We checked the trap the next morning and there was a cat in it. She looked a lot like one of the cats we had fixed last year, but this cat wasn't going to let us lift her tail to look. So off to the vet, and we did find out it was the cat from last year. Of course Dr. Richman had to knock her out to check, and yes, this time we had her ear tipped to easily identify her as a fixed cat.

For those of you not familiar with TNR, it was standard procedure to cut off the tip of the cat's ear so the colony caregiver could tell which ones were already fixed. That way what happened to us could be avoided. The cat was already unconscious for the surgery so it wasn't a painful procedure. From our observations the cats barely noticed at all, and the other cats in the colony didn't appear to ridicule them for their funky looking ears.

Since Dr. Richman had to sedate her to determine if he had already spayed her, we had to put her in the recovery building overnight. We wanted to make sure the cats recovered from the anesthesia before releasing them into the colony. We would let her out the next day and all would be well. Of course the entire time we were doing this, the one cat we still needed to catch, (Maggie's mom) was sitting out in the open watching us.

We returned the next day to let the cat out; the food was gone, the litter box had been used, but there was no sign of the cat. We checked the building again, no holes, broken windows or anything for the cat to escape from, yet we couldn't find the cat. Now granted, sometimes Bob and I couldn't remember if we turned off the lights or watered the plants, but we were pretty sure we remembered putting a cat in the building. We assumed someone else with a key to the building had released the cat. We checked with everyone who had keys, but no one confessed to letting the cat out. We checked the building again, but still no cat. We filled the food and water dishes, just in case she was still in the building, and went home.

We went back the next day and once again the food dish was empty (okay, it really was time for a sanity check). While I went to get more food, Bob really started searching the building. After banging on the empty shelves several times, he saw a "grey streak" run out from under the shelves and towards the feeding station.

The only plausible reason we could come up with for not finding the cat earlier was that she had been experimenting with some sort of "Alien Feline Particle Beam Matter Antimatter Transportation Device." Yep, you guessed it; this cat was a fan of *Star Trek*. At least we knew the cat was okay.

As we left the building, Maggie's mom was calmly watching the whole thing. We were starting to think she was having way too much fun outsmarting us.

Back at the townhouse things were moving forward with the kittens, but much slower than we would like.

Maggie had turned into quite the groomer. She would come up to Bob or me and start grooming our feet or our hands. Only now she was teething, meaning it was usually lick, lick, chomp. It was only really disturbing at 2 a.m. when we were sound asleep. We were hoping she would grow out of this phase in the real near future.

Then Maggie made a great discovery, the wonderful world of table scraps (hence her new nickname, Maggie the Mooch). She was relentless when we sat down to eat. When we had this problem with Ghost, we would simply throw her in the powder room until we were done eating. The powder room was no longer available, so a typical dinner would go something like this: Bob would sit down with a plate of food; Maggie would mount a frontal attack, Bob would say "no Maggie" and put her back on the floor. Unthwarted, she would sneak up from the side, using the "nuzzle under the arm" approach, which would land her back on the floor. By now I would arrive with my plate of food. So we were back to a frontal attack on my plate. Then Ghost would notice something was happening, and if Maggie could get away with it, so could she. The end result; Bob and I were considering eating in the closet.

Maggie's next adventure occurred on a Sunday, shortly after we moved Goldie and Grey from the powder room to the third bedroom. I was in the bedroom working on a sewing project (making aprons for Uncle Nicky's). I figured that would work well for all of us, the kittens would get some attention, and I would get something accomplished. Well that was the plan at least. What really happened was the kittens were so worn out from playing earlier in the day that they were dead to the world, sound asleep on the bed and had no interest in me.

Tia was hanging around outside the door knowing there was kitten food in the vicinity. And, like any good cat, she was following one of the official Rules of Cats: Something about anything on the other side of a closed door must be better than what was on their side of the door. The fact that the door to the bedroom was closed wasn't going to deter her. She started pawing and banging at the door. I finally relented and let her in, figuring she would never see the kittens, and hoping the kittens would sleep through the whole thing. Tia walked in, sniffed around, had some kitten food and was satisfied. What I didn't know was that she was just the "point cat" in an all-out Rude Cat ambush.

Before I go any further, let me explain something about Ashley, our number three and mostly Maine Coon kitty. Like most Maine Coons, the purpose of Ashley's body was merely to put a little distance between her six inch long whiskers and her rather impressive tail. She was also an incredible flirt, purring, mrupping, and chirping at anyone who would listen to what she had to say. Essentially, we were talking about the "blonde bimbo" of the feline world. As such, she didn't always consider the consequences of her actions; like coming to a stop from a full tilt run, or cornering on a tile floor. Lastly, anyone who spent any time around Ashley knew she was a shoulder kitty, that is, anyone even partially leaning over was fair game for her to launch onto their back and curl up on their shoulders.

Now back to the story.

As I opened the door to usher Tia out, Maggie ran into the room. As I bent over to grab Maggie, Tia doubled back into the room. Ashley took this opportunity to do her "shoulder cat leap" onto my back.

Now I was hunched over with Ashley on my back, Maggie cradled in one arm, attempting to reach down to catch Tia with the other hand. Then Maggie started batting at Ashley's tail. That didn't help Ashley's mood at all. Now I had two cats swatting at each other around my face. Billie Jo and Ghost took that opportunity to stroll past me and started munching on the kitten food. I didn't mind so much that they outsmarted me; I just didn't appreciate the gleeful look they gave me as they did it.

Despite these minor "incidents" our effort to socialize Maggie was going well. Our only problem was she would disappear if anyone else arrived at our townhouse. She just wasn't becoming the type of cat the average person wanted to adopt. That settled it; Bob and I officially adopted Maggie and make her a permanent member of our family. We bought her a collar and ordered an ID tag.

Then it was time for her first visit with our regular vet. Thankfully she was somewhat timid with Dr. Harrison; we only had to chase her around the exam room once, and she never even tried to bite him. The final diagnosis: healthy four month old kitten, but she had some roundworms and ear mites. So we were sent home with two syringes of deworming stuff (yeah, the yellow goop), instructions to clean out her ears every day and enough ear mite medicine to give her twice a day for the next two weeks.

We tried to give Maggie her deworming medicine as soon as we got home. She wasn't all that happy with us for taking her to the vet in the first place, so she was less than receptive to the idea of taking her medicine. At least I think we got a little of it into her. We also found out this stuff would make great mousse for both cat and human hair.

As for the ear mites, the cleaning out of a kitten's ears was not a job for the squeamish. Giving ear mite medicine to a kitten wasn't either. On our first attempt I gently held Maggie while Bob tried to put two drops of the medicine in each ear. On the next try, I held Maggie a little tighter. For the third try, we wrapped her in a towel. We finally settled on Maggie wrapped in a towel, scrunched between my knees, with Bob squirting some of the medicine at her and hoping it hit its mark. After that we only had twenty-seven more doses to go. It would have been helpful if Ashley, Billie Jo and Tia hadn't been snickering at us in the background.

Meanwhile, Hissor and Hissetta were still hanging out in the powder room and were reluctantly enjoying our visits with them. They really made a breakthrough when they discovered that Bob and I could make the ping pong balls move. We thought we had it made when they actually let us pet them. We had no idea a kitten could purr and hiss at the same time. I guess they sort of enjoyed our company, but didn't quite trust us yet. Maybe we would earn the rest of their trust soon.

Goldie and Grey were making progress too. They would actually run up to us for attention when we went into their room. Maybe they would be adoptable after all.

The last kitten was getting restless hanging out in the second bedroom with his mom. After all, his brothers and sisters were gone, and Momma Kitty was usually too busy glaring at Bob and me to play with him. Then one day Bob got him to play with an old telephone cable. He seemed to enjoy playing with the "string," but kept crashing into Momma Kitty. We're sure that did nothing to endear us to her.

On the trapping front we hit some hard times. Maggie's mom refused to cooperate despite our best efforts. We diligently kept setting the trap, hoping she would tire of the game and go into the trap just to get rid of us. Instead, we caught baby raccoons. We're not sure if Maggie's mom was tricking them into the trap, but we wouldn't put it past her. They were really cute, but Bob resisted the temptation to go into the raccoon rescue business and sent them scurrying back into the woods.

A few days later, Hissor and Hissetta stopped hissing at us. They even acted like they were looking forward to our visits (yeah, I know they were just playing us for the food, but hey, we were buying it). We decided to reunite them with Goldie and Grey (actually we just wanted the powder room back). The reunion went well; they played and played and finally ended the day sleeping in a pile 'o kittens under the bed.

Now we had four kittens that were getting pretty tame. It was time to work harder at finding them homes. We called several shelters and placement groups. The ones that would call us back said they were full, and pointed us to other groups that said the same. We learned there were far more cats and kittens in the world than there were available homes.

We thought we hit the jackpot one day when a lady called looking for kittens. She was referred to us by Dr. Harrison, and was interested in one, maybe two kittens. We arranged for her to visit the kittens and hoped they would behave. I think she would have been far more impressed if the kittens had come out from under the bed. She decided to keep looking for something a little more affectionate. I guess she wasn't looking for a project, just a sweet little kitten to cuddle up with her. We'd have to teach our little ones to be better at sucking up to people.

The Rude Cats seemed the most disappointed at the failed adoption. They felt Bob and I spent entirely too much time in the second and third bedrooms (at least we were spending too much time in these bedrooms without them). They began to express their displeasure by picking on Ghost. All Ghost had to do was walk by Ashley or Billie Jo and they would smack her on the butt. Ghost was big enough she could easily send either one flying, but instead she would run to Bob or me with a pathetic look. Being the softies that we were, we would immediately comfort her and make sure she got some treats. As these incidents started occurring more frequently, we became suspicious that Ghost orchestrated the whole thing to get the attention and the treats. Come to think of it, that was probably her plan all along.

Of course we were still setting the traps, working at Uncle Nicky's part-time, and working full-time at the Census Bureau. We were hoping to get some sleep in the near future. No one said the life of animal rescue would be easy.

The Great Kitten Capture

We finally had some excitement that had nothing to do with the cats. There were eight police cars in front of our townhouse one morning. We want to make it clear that the police were not responding to any kind of secret SOS or any other type of messages from Momma Kitty. Our next door neighbor, who just happened to be a police officer, hit Bob's car. Fortunately, Bob was completely innocent of any wrong doing (oh yeah, and nobody was hurt). He was just sitting in the car getting ready to head to work when a police cruiser came around the corner and hit him head on.

It turned out that when a police officer was in an accident (especially when she was a cute, young police officer), most of the other officers in the area wanted to stop by for "moral support." It was the Grand Central Station of police cruisers for a couple of hours. Fortunately, they completed their investigation and towed away the police cruiser. Bob drove away in our little Toyota MR2 with barely a scratch.

Now on with the adventures:

As we mentioned earlier, the fifth kitten (now called Brownie), was still with Momma Kitty in the second bedroom. He was getting bored and restless; after all, he was a three month old kitten with lots of energy. He wanted someone to run and play with him. Momma Kitty had no interest in these types of activities. She was still too busy plotting the end of the human race.

Brownie loved to play with the assorted phone cables Bob dangled in front of him, but he was still skittish about being handled. In a nutshell, he was getting better, but still not tame enough to be a pet for your average person. In order to finish working with him, we had to separate him from Momma Kitty. It appeared she was having a bad influence on his socialization with her plotting the end of the human race and all. We were planning how to separate him from Momma Kitty when he took matters into his own paws one morning. We opened the bedroom door to feed them and Brownie escaped. That was too easy!! All we had to do was catch him, and put him in the third bedroom with the rest of the kittens.

Once again luck was on our side. Ashley and Billie Jo were only twenty feet away, and were less than pleased to come nose to nose with another kitten. Apparently, two irritated, hissing females were too much for this little boy. He turned tail and ran right into our arms. Shortly after that he was romping around the third bedroom with his brothers and sisters. Although he was a little shy at first, Brownie settled down and started participating in all the kitty games. He also became quite affectionate with Bob and me, earning the title "Junior Lap Fungus."

Then the fall season was upon us and the kittens were ready to be "fixed" and given their rabies shots. In an act of either bravery or stupidity, we made an appointment for all the kittens on the same day. Our first obstacle was to take their food away the night before; at least our neighbors didn't call the police to report the loud kitty protests. Our next obstacle was getting the kittens to the vet. This task would have been easier if we had five kitty carriers and a large van to carry them in. However, we had three kitty carriers and Bob and I hadn't matured enough to drive anything bigger than a two-seater sports car. So we had to make do. Our plan was to put three kittens in the biggest carrier and the two remaining kittens would get stuffed into the next biggest carrier.

The kittens had started mounting coordinated escape attempts from their room, so we thought we would use that to our advantage. We figured all we had to do was put the carrier up to the door, open the door a crack and the kittens would run right into the carrier without thinking. At least it sounded like a good plan to Bob and me. What we forgot to consider was the "Emergency Rear Spring Activation System" that came as standard equipment on all cat models. That's right, instead of running full speed into the carrier; the kittens ran, sprang up and over the carrier and took off for parts unknown in the townhouse.

The next forty-five minutes resembled something of a three-ring circus. Bob and I chased the kittens around the townhouse. We would put one kitten in the carrier, catch another one, and when we put that one in the carrier, the first one would jump out and the chase would start again. The Rude Cats would run along side coaching the kittens on the best places to hide from us.

In the end, the kittens were all in their carriers, the carriers did fit in my car (yeah, I know we should have checked first), and Bob and I were even able to squeeze into the car too. By now we were completely exhausted. All that expended energy and we hadn't even left the townhouse yet. Even worse, we still had to stop by Uncle Nicky's and see if we had caught any cats last night.

Fortunately, the trap was empty (we usually were upset when the trap was empty, but we were really worn out by now and thought it was a good thing for a change). Now it was on to the vet with the kittens. Upon arrival we learned the vet's assistant wasn't there yet, but Dr. Richman was ready to start working on the cats. Could we assist him while he started neutering the male kittens? What choice did we have? It was another crash course on surgical procedures.

All went well, Bob didn't pass out, and the kittens were fixed and quietly recovered from their surgery.

By the end of the night, the kittens were up and running around, impervious to the fact they had just had surgery. Unfortunately, they still had a serious case of roundworms. To make matters worse, Maggie had been sneaking into their room to play, which meant although she had been treated for roundworms, she might have picked them up again. As Maggie shared litter boxes with the Rude Cats, she might have infected them too. We were pretty sure Momma Kitty also had roundworms. That meant another trip to the vet for more of the yellow goop. Dr. Harrison said the medicine tasted like egg custard and the cats would love it. I didn't bother to ask him how he knew what the medicine tasted like, I just accepted it. This time the staff didn't even try to fix us separate syringes of the medicine. They just handed us the bottle and a handful of syringes and said "good luck."

Although I wasn't looking forward to giving eleven cats various amounts of deworming medicine, I was determined to eradicate this parasite from our family. It was getting close to dinner time, so I figured I would just pop the medicine down the cats' throats, and then give them their dinner. I started with the kittens. Brownie came to me first; I caught him and got most of the goop into him. One small victory. Now on to the next kitten, Hissor. Well, I got most of it into him. By now the kittens were on to me, and were getting harder to catch. Goldie was the most interesting. Rather than swallow the medicine as I shot it into his mouth, he just let it run back out. I think I got some of it in him, but it was kind of hard to tell.

Now it was time to get the Rude Cats. I wasn't sure if it was the slightly crazed expression on my face or if the kittens had alerted them, but there wasn't a Rude Cat to be found. I tried running the can opener (the feline equivalent of the dog whistle), but no dice. They weren't falling for that one. I popped open a can of their favorite food. At least Maggie showed up. She was less than enthusiastic about taking more of the medicine, partially due to the fact she still hadn't finished cleaning the deworming medicine out of her fur from the last time. I managed to get most of the medicine inside her mouth, with just enough getting into her fur to make a little kitty Mohawk.

Now I had to change my strategy and go after specific cats. You see the amount of medicine given to the cat depended on the cat's weight. I had to pre-load my syringes accordingly, and chase down specific cats. I'm glad no one saw my "mad doctor" scene as I was chasing down the cats with my "evil medicine" in hand. I finally finished deworming everyone and could tentatively declare myself the victor in round one.

As I mentioned earlier, the kittens were getting bored with their room. To combat this they started mounting break out attempts whenever we opened their door. The kittens would usually only run into a bathroom or the master bedroom, and then come back in a few minutes.

On one such escape, Hissor got brave and ran down the steps to the main floor where he met Ghost, head on. Hissor had never seen a cat as big as Ghost. He stopped cold in his tracks and his eyes got big as saucers. In a complete panic Hissor took off at top speed through the living room, the dining room and into the kitchen where he promptly lost all footing on the vinyl floor. Ghost, who was totally fascinated by this miniature version of herself, was behind him all the way, further freaking him out. The harder he tried to get away from Ghost, the more his little paws skidded on the floor. Ghost, captivated by this display sat down to watch, which frustrated Hissor even more. By the time I caught up with him, he was more than happy to let me carry him back to his room.

Anyone Want a Kitten?

Bob and I had to get serious about finding homes for our kids or we would have to expand our townhouse. As luck would have it, two people Bob and I worked with were interested in getting a kitten for their daughters. It didn't take us long to seize the opportunity and introduce them to Brownie, our little junior lap fungus, cuddle bug. They fell in love with him right away and made him part of their family. Bob and I were saddened to see him go, but we knew he would get far more attention with four humans to dote over him than as one of eleven cats living with us. Bob and I said good-bye to him and carefully put him in his new carrier. He was scared, but behaving himself. As we carried him out to their car, we heard an incredibly loud series of meows. Startled, we looked at Brownie; no it wasn't him. The meows were coming from across the street. A little orange tabby kitten came running over to us meowing his head off. We named him Pumpkin and brought him into the townhouse. I guess the word was out we had an opening.

Pumpkin was in our new "quarantine room" in the basement. He started out in the powder room, but kept meowing so loudly that Bob and I couldn't get any sleep. He was about three months old, not fixed, but was so friendly; he had to belong to someone and was either dumped or escaped from them. We checked around the neighborhood, but nobody would claim the little guy.

Pumpkin was a sweet boy, but he was the loudest kitten we had ever encountered. He would start to wail continuously whenever he was left alone. In addition to upsetting all our other cats and kittens, he was beginning to disturb the neighbors. We just hoped we wouldn't be arrested for disturbing the peace. After all, we did have a police officer living next door. We had to find a solution and the quicker the better.

Bob and I had been volunteering at Save A Life, a local animal shelter, since Dr. Richman began doing the spay and neuter surgeries for our cats. The owners of the shelter, Bill and Janice, told us they could help place the kittens if we would socialize them and make sure all of their vet work was completed. We took them up on their offer after another sleepless night with Pumpkin. They agreed to hold him at their facility until we could find him a new home. We hated to do it, but couldn't survive any longer without sleep.

As part of our volunteering with Save A Life, we would soon get our first introduction to the phenomenon of cat shows. The cat shows had become a great adoption outlet for the shelter. They were similar to the dog shows, but with categories appropriate to cats. A lot of cat lovers attended these events and many were looking for new pets. The people running these shows were very rescue friendly and would invite rescue groups to the shows to help them find homes for the cats.

As luck would have it there was a CFA (Cat Fancier Association) cat show the following weekend in Chantilly, Virginia. Bill and Janice were taking about twenty cats and kittens from the shelter, and said we could bring Pumpkin and our remaining foster kittens, Goldie, Grey, Hissor, and Hissetta, to give them a shot at finding a home.

All we had to do was get the kids ready for the show and help with the adoptions. Bob and I took the kittens up to Save A Life the day before to get their final vaccinations and deworming treatments. We left the kittens at the shelter with the understanding they would ride to the show with the other cats in the morning. When Bob and I left that night, the kittens were in a cage looking scared and unhappy. It broke our hearts to leave them there, but we felt it would be best for them in the long run. We wanted to give the kids as much chance as possible to be adopted. Bob and I had a few things to do in the morning and wouldn't get to the cat show until close to lunch time.

It was time for the "best laid plans" myth to rear its ugly head. When Bob and I arrived at the cat show the next day, we were surprised to find our kittens hadn't made the trip. Bill and Janice said our sweet little kittens managed to get their cage door open and were running loose around the shelter. The kittens were so talented at escape and evasion techniques that the five volunteers trying to catch them didn't have a chance. The volunteers finally ran out of time and had to pack up the rest of the cats and head to the show. Bill said this was one of the few times in their history that a kitten had managed to get the cage door open. Bob and I weren't sure whether to be proud of our kittens' ingenuity, or embarrassed by all the trouble they caused. Overall, the show was a huge success for the shelter, with over forty cats and kittens finding homes over the weekend. We just wished some of them had been ours.

After the show, we made the trip back to the shelter, rounded up our little troublemakers and brought them back to our townhouse for more intensive behavioral training.

A few weeks later, our foster kids – Pumpkin, Goldie, Grey, Hissor, and Hissetta and thirty other adoptable cats went to another cat show, this time at the state fairgrounds in Timonium, Maryland. All the kittens handled the show well, with Pumpkin being by far the most entertaining. He would reach out of his cage and grab people. We wished we could train all the cats to work the crowd like that. Three of our kids, Hissor, Hissetta and Pumpkin, were adopted along with twenty other cats and kittens from the shelter. Bill and Janice felt it was just a matter of time until the right people were found for Goldie and Grey. They offered to keep them at the shelter to give them a chance to be seen by more people. We controlled our emotions and went home without them, hopeful we would soon find a home for our last two "foster children."

It partially worked. Grey found a home a few days later. Although Bob and I weren't there to say good-bye to her, the volunteers at the shelter said she went to a very nice family. They were almost sorry to see her go. She had become a serious "cuddle bug," always running to the front of the line to make sure she got her share of ear scritches and tummy rubs. Goldie was still hanging out at the shelter waiting for his chance at a new home.

We also got an update on Hissetta and she was doing well in her new home and was happily playing with her new big kitty brother. It was bittersweet for Bob and me to see our kids going to new homes. It was what we wanted for them, but we missed them once they left. It was amazing how fast you could get attached to these little buggers.

Now we were back to working with Momma Kitty and trying to find a home for our last foster kitten, Goldie. It turned out Momma Kitty had decided not to do away with Bob, me and the rest of the human race after all. She was still spending most of her time hiding between the desk and the wall or behind the printer, but Momma Kitty had gone from a snarling, hissing, "touch me and I'll shred you" attitude to a "maybe I'll come out, but don't forget to scratch my chin" type of cat.

Bob was petting her one night when I went into the second bedroom to check on her. Bob, being the dutiful husband, stopped petting her while he was talking to me. After a while, Momma Kitty stuck her head out from behind the printer and gave us both a "HEY!! You're ignoring me!!!" type of look. She was definitely making progress towards becoming a wonderful pet; we just had to be patient. At this point, we had given up on returning her to the feral colony. We just couldn't bring ourselves to put her back after working with her for the last couple of months. I guess we were failing at the trap/neuter/release program. I think the key was to release them right away before getting attached.

Cali Leads us to Boomer

Goldie spent the next five months living full-time at Save A Life and began sharing duties with their mascot Bones. We went there every weekend to help with adoptions and to hopefully find Goldie a forever home.

Bones, the Save A Life mascot, was a cat Bill came across while at a local animal control facility several years earlier. Bones was left behind in an apartment when his family moved out and was almost dead when someone finally found him. They were getting ready to put him to sleep at the animal control facility when Bill happened to walk by. He immediately felt a connection to Bones and asked if they would release the cat to him and give him a shot at saving his life. Of course they were happy to give the little guy a chance.

Bill brought Bones home and spent the next few weeks slowly nursing him back to health. He finally made a full recovery and became a fixture at the shelter. He was known as "A Bag of Bones" during his recovery; hence the shortened version of the name that stuck with him throughout the rest of his life.

Bones always greeted Bob and me when we arrived at the shelter. He had a habit of climbing up your leg if you didn't show him the proper amount of attention. He made it virtually impossible to ignore his demands. We really didn't mind and usually spent more time with him than any other cat at the shelter, even our boy Goldie.

By now we were through the Christmas and New Years holidays and well into the spring of 1998. The cats in residence, Tia, Billie Jo,

Ashley, Ghost, and Maggie, had finally adjusted to each other. Even Momma Kitty was beginning to settle down and become a really nice cat. Life was becoming normal again, but apparently a little too quiet, which only meant one thing: we got a call. There were a bunch of kittens living on a McDonald's parking lot in Dunkirk, Maryland. They were running into traffic and becoming something of a nuisance. A few of the employees felt bad for them and were worried something was going to happen to the kittens. Could Bob and I help?

We were lucky in one respect; someone else was willing to trap the cats, but she couldn't keep them and work with them. That's where Bob and I came into the picture. Okay, we could take one, maybe two of the kittens. Well, there were four kittens; could we take them all? How could we say no? The third bedroom was cat free now, so what the heck.

The next day we took custody of the four older kittens, one smoky grey, two black and white tuxedos and a little calico (code named Blue, Blackie, Abbey and Cali). The good news: they weren't totally wild. The bad news: they were at least six months old, meaning they would be harder to tame, and harder to place into permanent homes. They were pretty good at hissing and hiding, but at least they responded to the attention we were giving them.

Cali Ready to Party at the Townhouse

The Rude Cats took the latest additions in stride, copping a "just give us the kitten food or the couch would be the new scratching post" type of attitude. I guess they were starting to accept the constant flow of foster kids at our townhouse.

However, the socializing wasn't going as well as it did with Momma Kitty's litter. These kittens were much better at hiding. We spent the first few days "plugging" holes in an attempt to keep the kittens from pulling their vanishing act: under the sewing machine, under the dresser and the all impressive "in the box spring." We really wanted to take the bed apart anyway, and shaking a few kittens out of the box spring seemed a good enough reason. After that, the kittens went vertical. That's right; they slept in the curtains. I was pretty sure it was a rude awakening (no pun intended) for the kittens sleeping in the curtains when they came crashing down. At least we now knew how Ghost pulled off her disappearing act in this room. It never occurred to us to check inside the curtains over the window. I guess she could still keep her name even though we now knew her secret. She answered to it and she really did earn it.

So far Bob and I had been lucky to have healthy, low maintenance cats, and then it happened. We started to hit a run of bad luck with infections.

Ashley started sneezing. Okay, one upper respiratory infection (the feline version of a cold). Normally the vet wouldn't prescribe anything for it and would just let it run its course; but because we had so many cats, we would start Ashley on antibiotics just to play it safe.

At least the pink medicine showed up really well on Ashley's tabby striping. Not to be outdone, Momma Kitty also developed an infection, in both ears. That could be a problem; Momma Kitty's last visit to the vet was in a wire trap right after we caught her. From her point of view, it was a less than pleasant experience. We knew she wouldn't be thrilled with another visit to the vet. We were just as confident she wouldn't be thrilled when the vet tech flushed her ears.

Fortunately, Momma Kitty and the vet tech survived and we were sent home with more antibiotics. This came in handy, as Ashley was generous enough to give her cold to Maggie. Maggie announced this at about 3 a.m. by sneezing and hacking on Bob, me, and several of the other cats.

By now, the new set of foster kittens had been with us for about ten days. They were still hiding, but not hissing and growling as much. One night I noticed the little calico (Cali) had thrown up a lot and didn't seem to feel too well. I attributed it to having just puked up most of her dinner. The next night I found out otherwise. When I checked on the kittens, the tuxedos and the smoky grey kitten were hiding in their normal spots, but the calico was nowhere to be seen. I finally found her, comatose under the bed. We put her into a kitty carrier and hustled off to the emergency vet.

After drawing blood and doing some basic tests, it was determined she had a massive viral infection and that yes, she could be saved, but it wouldn't be easy, or cheap. We left the emergency vet with instructions to do whatever was necessary to save her and a copy of our credit card. We were told to call back at 4 a.m. for an update.

At 4 a.m. (yes, we did actually wake up for this) she was still alive and in an oxygen tent. She was going to survive the night!!! Just come in at 6 a.m. to pick her up. Unfortunately, we didn't have a twenty-four hour emergency vet in the area yet. That posed a more immediate problem, what to do with a very sick, contagious cat at six in the morning? Our regular vet wasn't open yet, and the emergency vet was closing down and had to get all the overnight patients out. So, being the decisive, ready for action types, we had Cali's IVs capped off, called in to work late with a "family" emergency, and drove around trying to figure out what to do with Cali.

When we finally arrived at our vet, Cali's diagnosis was confirmed. She was a very sick kitty, and still wasn't out of the woods. She was immediately taken to their intensive care area for more antibiotics and IV fluids. We found out we had another problem. Their overnight person, who usually monitored the intensive care area, had just quit. Could we come back at closing time (around 6 p.m.) to pick up Cali and take her back to the emergency vet? So much for convenience.

The next morning Bob and I managed to drag ourselves out of bed in time to get Cali by the 6 a.m. pick up deadline. Cali was slowly gaining strength and could pick her head up and look around a little bit. She was even trying to stand. That was a vast improvement over the almost comatose kitty we dropped off the night before. She still needed continuous antibiotics and nutritional support through an IV tube, meaning back to our vet. By now we were on a first name basis with everyone there.

We had some time to kill before we could drop Cali off at our vet, so we went to look at a couple of land parcels for sale in the area. A few months earlier we had begun a quest to find a property where we could start our own animal sanctuary. We wanted to help more animals, but definitely didn't have the space or zoning for it at the townhouse. We were already pushing things with all the animals we were fostering.

On the way to the properties we saw a small animal in the middle of the road. It kept running down the road ignoring all the cars that were honking and driving around it. At first we couldn't tell if it was a cat or a dog. All we could tell was it was small and not too bright. That was when our soft spot for animals kicked in (okay, the word sucker came to mind). We pulled over and found out it was a small dog. He promptly ran towards us and sat down directly in front of the car. Okay, maybe the dog was smarter than we thought. He was determined to get help and wasn't going to let a little thing like a 3,000 pound car stop him.

Bob picked him up and looked him over; it was a Miniature Pinscher. He appeared to be in good shape and didn't have any signs of injuries. He also didn't have any identification and didn't show any signs that he had been wearing a collar recently. The little guy couldn't have weighed more than eight pounds. Even though he had no tags or identification, he had been neutered, so at some point he must have been someone's pet.

There he was in the middle of nowhere, and we didn't think he would last too long on his own, especially the way he was running down the middle of the road. Not knowing what else to do, and still having some time to kill before dropping Cali off, we threw him in the car and went looking for "lost dog" signs. We didn't find any, leaving us to believe he was dumped by his former family.

Now we had two problems: a very sick cat and a homeless dog.

The problem with Cali was easier to fix. We dropped her off at the vet with what were becoming the usual instructions (keep pumping fluids and antibiotics into her). The problem with the dog was more difficult. We brought him home and pondered over this one a little more.

We knew it may not have been the brightest idea to bring a dog with an unknown history into a house with ten cats, but we figured even if the dog did go after the cats, they had those razor sharp instruments of death: claws, and if that didn't work, they could easily jump up on the furniture to get away from the little guy. Besides, with the exception of Cali, all our cats were bigger than him.

The initial meeting between the little dog and the Rude Cats was interesting. We put the dog in the living room as soon as we got home. Ghost, who had been sleeping on the back of the couch, was the first on the scene. She cautiously peered down at the dog and looked up as if to say "not only did you bring another cat home, but this one's a MUTANT!!!" Billie Jo was the next on the scene. She approached him from the side, until he turned around and started to sniff her. She let out her standard "touch me and I'll shred you" hiss and jumped straight up onto the TV. This kind of impressed the dog.

Soon Maggie and Ashley were closing in from both sides. The dog made an attempt to sniff Ashley's butt, which apparently in dog language was considered a polite introduction. This form of introduction in cat language didn't translate the same way, at least not to Ashley. She explained this to the dog with extreme clarity. Soon the dog realized that everywhere he looked, there was a cat looking back at him. He was starting to get a little nervous; okay, he was starting to get a lot nervous.

We thought things had settled down, and then Tia, the high ruler of the Rude household, made her entrance. Anyone who had ever met Tia, or who knew anything about our past experiences, knew her Royal Highness ran the house. Bob and I were only there to pay the bills, clean out the litter boxes and work the can opener. Tia rendered her opinion of the newcomer. As always her ruling was swift and unquestionable. She went up to him, looked him over, let out a huge "don't mess with me" hiss and gave him a good swat on the nose. That was enough for the little dog. He turned tail and hid behind Bob on the couch. At least he seemed to have the proper respect for the cats.

It was time to give the little guy a name. We always had a hard time coming up with appropriate names for most of the animals. We usually waited for them to do something that triggered a name for them. Boomer did this in a rather unattractive way. It may have been the swat from Tia, maybe the plentiful food, maybe even the stress of a new house, but shortly after the incident with Tia, he left a nice big deposit in the middle of the kitchen floor. Man that was one big "Boomer" for a little dog. The name stuck. Fortunately, the habit didn't.

Boomer the Miniature Pinscher

Now that we had solved the homeless dog problem, we returned to the very sick cat dilemma. Fortunately, Cali made it through the day at the vet and was slowly improving. She still needed continuous antibiotics and IV fluids, but she was getting slightly better. Her major problem now was that she refused to eat. That meant she still needed twenty-four hour care that included receiving nutrition via a feeding tube. The people caring for her said she was starting to raise a "ruckus" when put back in her cage. We thought that was a good sign. It was better to have some spunk than to be flat out on the floor.

The next day, Cali was judged well enough to be out of immediate danger and released to us for home care. She still needed several antibiotics and hadn't started eating yet, which meant Bob and I would not only have to start "pilling" Cali, we would also have to force feed her using the feeding tube. It was time for another crash course in critical care.

A typical feeding/medicating session with Cali would go something like this: Bob and I would load up our feeding tube with a special mixture of food and nutritional supplements. We would get the required pills ready. We would cover the furniture with plastic drop cloths. We would then get five or six towels ready. We would retrieve Cali from her quarantine room (the powder room) and prepare ourselves for battle. One of us would put Cali in a headlock and hold her mouth open. The other one would try to "pop" the pill down her throat. On the second try, we would put her on the floor, hold her with our knees, pry her mouth open, and then "pop" the pill down her throat. By the third try we usually had success or had to start all over again.

Then we had to feed her. Eventually Bob and I wised up and started wearing clothes that were roughly the same color as the food we were feeding her. Considering how sick and weak Cali was, she sure managed to put up a good fight when it came to taking her medicine and food.

It took another ten days, but Cali finally made a complete recovery from her "near death" ordeal. She still wanted to be a spoiled rotten baby though. She also felt this experience entitled her to get away with a lot more with regards to the other cats (like stealing toys, food, and launching sneak attacks). For the most part, she was able to pull it off! Every time another cat started to get mad at her antics, Cali would rub up against them and roll over onto her back. Even Billie Jo and Tia hadn't been able to bring themselves to smack her when she pulled her cute kitten act.

We don't want to forget about Boomer, the official first dog of the Rude Cats. Yes, we decided it was pointless to put Boomer up for adoption and made him a permanent member of our family. It was also nice having a dog around the townhouse to break up the monotony of caring for the cats (I think Bob just wanted to look macho walking this little eight pound puppy around the neighborhood).

Boomer was starting to settle into his new life among all the Rude Cats. He learned not to run up to the cats and to stay out of the trash. His one big problem, we didn't have any dog toys. He watched the cats play with shoe strings and would look at us with an "I don't get it" expression. So like proud new dog parents, Bob and I headed to our local PetSmart for dog toys. We carefully selected several fleece and plastic chew toys and a "state of the art" chew rope for him.

When we arrived at home, we placed our carefully chosen toys in front of Boomer. He looked at the assortment of toys and looked back at us with a "you still don't get it" look. The toys appeared to be about the right size when we were at the store, but the rope, pork chop and the other toys were too big for Boomer to get his mouth around. So Boomer was back to playing with borrowed kitty toys (by now he was into the cats for about eight furry mice).

Soon it was time for Boomer to visit Dr. Harrison for a check up and booster vaccinations. When we first found him, we took him to Dr. Richman and said "make him legal," which meant give him a rabies vaccination and make sure he was neutered. Now he needed the rest of his shots. On the appointed day, we dutifully took him to the clinic. The part where the vet tech weighed the dog went okay. Then it was time to take his temperature. If you've ever had a pet, you know which end the temperature was taken from. Let's just say we started with Boomer standing on the exam table, business end facing the technician. By the time the technician was able to get a reading, Boomer was standing on Bob's shoulder, and his eyes were HUGE. Then it was time for the shots. Did you know it took four people, in addition to the vet, to give shots to a Miniature Pinscher?

The Quest for a Sanctuary

Things started to quiet down a bit at the townhouse, which could only mean one thing: another cat must be on its way to us. This one came to us from a coworker. He was moving to a new apartment that didn't allow pets. His cat Junior either had to go to us or he would be dropped off at the local animal control. We took him in and scheduled him for his initial visit with Dr. Richman. He had never seen a vet before, so he was in for the "whole works."

Junior also marked a turning point in our animal rescue effort; he would be the last cat we took in before throwing caution to the wind, pulling up stakes and heading for larger quarters. (Although Junior marked a turning point, he was only with us a short time and then was adopted by a very nice family that wanted a sweet, loveable cat.) We wanted to expand our efforts to help animals, but were very limited from our townhouse. We had spent the last twelve months trying to find a property so we could pursue our dream of starting an animal sanctuary.

We thought we had found that piece of land several months ago, but ran into an unscrupulous realtor who accepted multiple contracts on the same property, essentially selling the same property multiple times. We weren't sure if the realtor was completely incompetent or simply a con artist trying to pull a scam on everyone. Either way, we were third in line to buy the property and ended up on the short end of the stick.

In January of 1999, we decided it was now or never and it was time to really commit ourselves to finding the right property. We called our realtor and put our townhouse up for sale. If you have ever tried to sell a house, you know there are certain things you can do to make the house more appealing. At a minimum the house should be incredibly clean, picked up, smelling good, with the beds made, towels folded and a minimum of clutter. Our townhouse usually failed on all counts. Let's face it: the only way we were going to sell our townhouse was to move out first.

As luck would have it, the family renting the two bedroom condo I bought after college was moving out in January. The timing seemed right, so we decided to move into the condo while we looked for the right property to start an animal sanctuary. We really hoped it wouldn't take too long; things could get really cramped with all our stuff and all the animals packed into a small condo.

Fortunately, we had enough stuff to minimally furnish the condo and still make the townhouse look fully furnished (okay, sometimes it was an advantage to have a lot of crap). As an added bonus, we could fix up the condo while we were living there. At least that was the game plan.

What we found at the condo changed our plans a little bit. The condo looked like a tornado had hit it. The carpet was covered in cat poop and red Kool-Aid. Bob and I were definitely cat lovers, but we had to draw the line at cat-poop carpeting. We might have been able to steam clean everything else out of the carpeting, but nothing was going to get rid of the red Kool-Aid.

Okay, so we had to replace the carpet and clean the place, no, fumigate the place. It would delay our move a little, but it would still be a great place to live while we looked for our new home. The carpet was ordered, and the condo was gutted and scrubbed; then we started painting.

During all of this, we were still working at Uncle Nicky's and volunteering at the Save A Life animal shelter (oh yeah, and we still had our full-time jobs at the Census Bureau, which was funding our animal rescue habit). We were beginning to think we would never sleep again.

The "big" day eventually arrived. It was time to move to the condo. The game plan was carefully prepared; I would go to the condo, finish painting the bathroom, and supervise the installation of the carpeting, while Bob stayed at the townhouse and steam cleaned the carpet. We figured these tasks would be completed by mid-afternoon, and we would begin the migration of furniture and animals to the condo that night (hey, it seemed like a good plan to us).

On my side of things, I discovered carpet installers take a lot of bathroom breaks. I was reminded of this every five minutes, usually just long enough to get the paint roller loaded and climb back up on the ladder. I would climb back down, leave the bathroom and then start all over again. Maybe I should have just hidden their coffee thermos.

Meanwhile, Bob was busy steam cleaning the townhouse. We knew a lot of people steam cleaned their carpet and it wasn't a big deal. Bob had an additional force working against him, Boomer the Min Pin. He still wasn't sure exactly where he fit in with our family. He was starting to get really apprehensive with our impending move. His whole world was suddenly changing and he wasn't sure if he was part of the game plan. After all, it wasn't that long ago he had been abandoned in the middle of the road.

Boomer definitely had a few anxiety issues. He dealt with these issues the only way he knew how; he started marking everything. I guess he thought if he couldn't be there to guard his stuff, at least others would know he had been there. He started peeing on boxes, walls, bedspreads, and at one point he even tried to "mark" a cat (Ghost really wasn't pleased when that happened).

Bob wasn't all that happy when he finished the steam cleaning and discovered Boomer's indiscretions. Now that Bob had the carpet cleaned, he had to go back to get all of Boomer's mishaps.

Back at the condo, I finally managed to kick the carpet installers out of the bathroom long enough to finish painting. Now my problem was the installers weren't exactly moving at the speed of light. As a matter of fact, it was amazing how long it was taking them considering the rooms were square, and there were no steps or furniture in the way. At least I was becoming well versed on everyone's love life (or lack thereof).

51

It was now late afternoon, and the carpet installers were still installing. They were inching their way towards the last room when they made a startling discovery; they were eight inches short of carpet. How did I want to deal with this? (Apparently they didn't think strangling them was a viable option.)

Well what did they think? I wanted them to finish the job with a piece of carpet the right size, not something pieced together from their mistakes. They would have to come back and finish the job in two weeks. They were grumbling about the inconvenience until they took one look at me, and decided it wouldn't be so inconvenient after all. This wasn't a show stopper; at least we had mostly new carpet. We just needed a small strip of carpeting in the dining room to finish things off. Meanwhile, Bob finally arrived at the condo with a load of furniture and our little boy Boomer (he didn't trust Boomer enough to leave him alone at the townhouse after his earlier indiscretions). It was amazing how fast carpet installers could move when threatened with the possibility of helping move furniture. They were in their van and gone almost before the front door closed.

Once the furniture was unloaded, we still had to get the now mystified and somewhat cranky Rude Cats moved to the condo. As anyone who had ever tried to get an uncooperative cat into a carrier knew, that operation came in a close second to giving a cat a bath. Multiply that by ten cats and we were going to have the equivalent of a skunk wandering onto a crowded football field, complete and utter chaos would be an understatement. We did some quick math. We had ten cats; we had seven kitty carriers. No matter how you computed it, the numbers just didn't work out.

We really didn't have any other options; the townhouse was going up for sale the next day and we had to be ready. After all, Bob and I were occasionally optimists, so we had high hopes we might get lucky and have a showing the first day.

We began preparations to get the cats into the carriers. We lined the carriers up in the garage, put on our heavy jackets and gloves, and then checked with the local blood bank to make sure they had our blood type. Our game plan was to quietly pick up each cat, lovingly carry them to the garage, and then stuff them into a carrier. Using this method we hoped the rest of the cats wouldn't be suspicious when it was their turn. It seemed like a good plan to us.

It was time to start the great cat move. The foster cats, Abbey, Blackie and Blue, were easy; they were already secluded in a room. They also would fit in one carrier (yes, Bob got to carry that one). Three down, seven to go. Ghost and Momma Kitty, being of more trusting natures were the next to be stuffed. Then Tia grudgingly allowed herself to be put in a carrier.

Now we had a problem: we had four cats to go and three carriers. We would put Maggie and Cali into a carrier together. In addition to being the two smallest cats, they also played together all the time. We hoped that meant they wouldn't kill each other during the ten minute trip to the condo. However, we had a little trouble with the logistics of putting two energetic cats in one carrier. Cali went in, Maggie went in, and then Cali came out. On the third round we finally tricked both cats into the carrier by throwing catnip, treats and a can of tuna into the carrier ahead of them. Now we just had the sisters, Billie Jo and Ashley.

Anyone who had ever met Billie Jo and Ashley thought they were beautiful, loving cats (okay, some people know otherwise; after all, Billie Jo did con the pet sitter into hand feeding her sardines one time). Getting these two into carriers was something akin to playing roller hockey without protective gear. Ashley usually required the towel-wrap, butt-drop method. Grab cat. Wrap in towel. Stand carrier upright and wedge it against the wall. Drop cat in butt first. Slam door shut. Seek medical attention for wounds. Once in the carrier, she could produce the most uncatlike vocalizations known to man, and she did this rather loudly. Ashley would be the last to be loaded.

Now we had to get Billie Jo. Stuffing Billie Jo into a carrier can sometimes take on aspects of all out gorilla warfare. We typically closed all the doors in the townhouse, trapped her in a room, preferably one without carpet, and then went through multiple gyrations to stuff her into the carrier. Did I mention we also bought a special top loading carrier for her? Worked great!

Now it was Ashley's turn. We prepared to do battle with our toughest rival. We prepared the towels, put on the heavy gloves and even had the carrier wedged in a corner of the garage. When we turned around to begin our capture of Ashley, she was already curled up in the carrier. I guess she knew we meant business, or was worried she would be left behind. All that prep work and worry for nothing.

Now that every critter was loaded up, we made our way to the condo. We were able to move them inside under the cover of darkness. You see, technically we were only allowed to have a maximum of four pets in this neighborhood. Anyone watching us move in could tell we were a bit over that limit. If caught we planned to use one of two excuses: either most of the cats were just visiting, or well, it was really the same cat; it's just the different lighting that's giving the illusion of different cats. Fortunately, the topic never came up. The move was over, Bob and I still had most of our blood and the neighbors had no idea how many animals we were harboring in our condo. We called it a success!

Blue only stayed with us a short time after we moved to the condo. She found a home with a young lady the following week. Although Blue now had a new life, she stayed true to her roots by helping her new mom eat an order of McDonald's French fries on the way home. For those of you who don't remember, Blue and her sisters were originally rescued from a McDonald's parking lot.

Fortunately, the rest of the Rude Cats were adjusting to their temporary home. Ghost and Maggie shared the computer hutch, while Momma Kitty claimed "under the bed" as her domain. Tia took over the laundry basket while Cali felt the entire house belonged to her. Billie Jo and Ashley took over the kitchen window, where they had hissing battles with Casper, the flame point Himalayan cat from next door. Casper was fascinated by the other cats and animals (Boomer didn't faze him at all). We lost count of the number of times we looked out a window and saw Casper staring back at us. We were quite grateful he couldn't talk and "spill his guts" about what he saw.

Now that we were settled into the condo, it was back to an all-out house hunting quest. We were prepared to spend months looking for the right property. We had already spent more than a year looking for this mystical place and hadn't found anything close to what we wanted in our price range.

Then our luck changed. Only three days after moving into the condo, Bob and Momma Kitty (she always hung out on the desk when

Bob was searching the web) came across a listing that had possibilities: The house was three years old, on five acres, really big, had hardwood floors, a gourmet kitchen, and no homeowner's association. It was in an area we liked, and was priced much less than we expected to pay for this type of property, which led us to the following question: What was wrong with it?

We called our realtor and told her we were interested in this house. She looked it up and asked the same question: what was wrong with it? Still it looked like a good deal, so we made an appointment and joked about checking for blood stains under the carpet.

The tour of the house was an unusual experience. We checked the yard for signs of recent digging activities, glowing objects or anything else out of place. The yard needed some work, but was an average looking lawn.

Then the plaque beside the door slowed us down a little; it read "Institute of Spiritual Technology." The people in the house slowed us down a little more. You see, when we drove up and were walking around the house, we could see people moving around inside the house, but nobody came out to greet us. No big deal, we would do the walk through and leave them alone.

Then we knocked on the door and there was no answer. We could still see and hear people moving around inside the house; they just weren't opening the door. Just as our realtor got ready to open the door herself, the door appeared to open all by itself. Expecting a person on the other side of the door, our realtor started to say hello and introduce herself. Then she realized she was talking to thin air. The people we saw walking around inside the house had disappeared. Okay, so it was starting to resemble a scene from the old TV show *The Addams Family*. We preferred to think that someone opened the door and then disappeared into the house rather than some of the other possibilities that ran through our minds.

We went ahead with the walk through to see what the house had to offer. We realized the house was close to perfect for our needs. We also discovered the people we saw in the house were hiding in the garage. At least we knew we weren't going crazy. They had experienced some problems selling the property the year before and were convinced using their house as a temple was the reason. They thought it might help sell the house if they made themselves scarce when potential buyers came over. At least that was a better explanation than some of the scenarios we had contemplated.

They told us the house was being used as the Eastern Regional Headquarters for the Hari Krishna's. They had statues of their "leader" all over the house. The most interesting room was the "temple room." This was where their "deities" were kept on a couple of alters. The area around the alter was painted with large golden peacocks (at least there was an animal connection). When we told them our plans for the house, they thought it was a great idea.

We finished our tour and met with the realtor in the driveway. She told us to think about it overnight and let her know if we wanted to put a contract on the house. Bob and I just looked at each other and immediately signed the contract while still in the driveway. The property wasn't exactly what we were looking for, but it was the closest we had seen in over a year. We didn't want to take a chance that someone would scoop it out from under us like our last experience trying to buy a property. It also helped that their asking price was already far below the market value.

Several days later we got some good news. The contract we put on the house was accepted; we had ten days to get things rolling. The home inspection was scheduled and we started the fun process of looking for a loan.

By the way, Bob and I were still working part-time at Uncle Nicky's, but with moving and volunteering at the animal shelter, we had dropped back to "emergency only" status.

During the home inspection my beeper went off: It was Uncle Nicky's; one waitress had called in sick, how soon could I get there? Half an hour later Bob's beeper went off: Uncle Nicky's again; the cook called in sick, could Bob work? A few minutes later, both of our beepers went off: Bob's sister Linda had gone into labor and Bob's mom, who was also working at the restaurant as a waitress, had to leave to take care of Linda's son Kyle. Things were getting desperate now, how long would it take us to get there? I guess this qualified under the "emergency only" status.

We hastily finished the home inspection and headed to the restaurant. Halfway through the dinner rush our realtor showed up at the restaurant; not to try Bob's cooking, but with a contract on the townhouse! At least we were getting a lot accomplished that night.

Linda accomplished a lot that night too; she had a little baby girl a few hours later. The baby even waited until everyone was through working for the night before entering the world. Bob and I now had a little niece named Jill to go with our nephew Kyle.

Bob and I felt we had a very productive day: we had a contract on the townhouse we were selling, we had a contract on the house we were buying, the new house had been inspected, we found a loan for the new house, our new niece arrived, and we made a couple hundred bucks at the restaurant.

We managed to get all the planets to align and had both houses tentatively scheduled to close at the end of April. That gave us seven weeks to finish packing the townhouse, move the fish pond, and find renters for the condo we were living in. It looked like everything was coming together as planned. We thought all was going well with our world, but then again Bob and I were occasional optimists.

Now back to reality. It was proving difficult to find renters for our condo. Anyone who has ever tried to find a renter could tell you what a parade of characters can show up claiming to be decent, law-abiding and more importantly, on-time, bill-paying people. Our latest odyssey into the landlord realm was no exception.

We ran an ad and were pleasantly surprised when we received our first call to set up an appointment for 11 a.m. the next day. By the time Bob and I went to work at Uncle Nicky's that night, we had three more appointments. In all, more than thirty people called about renting the condo. Now we had to start showing it. That was when things got interesting.

The reason we moved out of the townhouse was because Bob and I were too messy and clutter-oriented to live in a house being shown to prospective buyers. Additionally, having eleven animals lying around didn't help either. Showing a condo to potential renters fell into the same category.

The first potential renters were a prime example: The condo had been scrubbed, everything that could be packed into a box was packed to get it out of the way, litter boxes were cleaned and hidden in closets, and the cats swore they wouldn't use the litter boxes while people were there. The first prospective renters arrived. It was a couple with a four year old son. Okay, a family; they should be fairly responsible.

They looked at the condo and appeared to like it. Then it happened: Boomer emerged, and the lady shrieked in terror. It turned out she was afraid of dogs. By now the cats wanted to know what was going on, and started coming out of the wood work. The lady was also afraid of cats. The rest was history. We think she stopped hyperventilating sometime the next day.

The parade of nut cases continued for several days. We finally settled on a couple who were getting married in May. He was a computer programmer and she was a graduate student. Neither one of them were keen on animals, but hey, we were taking them with us. Plus, they gave us a check for the security deposit and the first month's rent and it didn't bounce. We were good to go on the rental front.

Things were also moving forward with the townhouse we were selling. The inspection was completed and it only turned up a few minor things: our doorbell didn't work and we had a leaky window. We could deal with those minor repairs.

We were finally given a definite settlement date for both houses at the end of April. The buyer's financing wasn't definite, but it was looking good. Now our only problem was how to move the fish in the pond behind the townhouse. We could have left them, but the new owners had no interest in the pond.

We came to the realization that planning a move in the month of April, when income taxes were due, was a major mistake. Where did we pack our tax receipts, investment documents, and tax forms? It had to be Bob's fault, after all, what good was a husband if you couldn't blame him for everything? Rather than spend hours looking through hundreds of boxes, we remembered this thing called an "extension." We had never tried it before, but figured this was as good a time as any to check into it. We requested an extension using "clueless" as the reason and hoped they would accept it. That bought us until August to move, find our documents and file our tax returns.

We started working on a plan to move the fish to the new house. We obviously needed to pack them up, but what would we use to transport them? They didn't make fish carriers, but we had a plan. We would buy enough Rubbermaid storage containers to hold all our fish.

We did get a strange look from the Kmart cashier when we bought twenty extra large plastic storage boxes and told her they were for the fish. I guess that wasn't an advertised use for the containers.

Now it was time to give some thought to getting our stuff from the assorted houses and into the new house. We had stuff stashed at the townhouse we were selling, the condo we were living in and Bob's sister's house. We figured we would need a really big truck. We called a couple of moving companies and they agreed, we did need a really big truck. They wanted over $2,000 to move us. Bob and I were too cheap (we liked to call it frugal) to fork out that much money. We decided to do it the old fashioned way: rent a truck, and bribe people to help us move with the promise of food and beer later. The word "later" was the key word. We had learned from experience, if you offered the food too early, the productivity of the helpers declined rapidly.

If you have ever looked through the phone book for rental trucks, the ads usually stated how big the trucks were, and approximately how many rooms the truck would hold. First off, we went for the biggest truck we could get; a twenty-eight footer. Second, those ads were very misleading; I guess they assumed minimally furnished rooms. Bob and I had a lot of stuff. We also discovered if you want to rent a truck near the end of the month, you better reserve it at the beginning of the month. We finally found a local Ryder rental company with a truck in our size.

Things were still going well with regards to selling the townhouse, but they were not going as well with the house we were buying. The sellers were being uncooperative. They might not have all their stuff out by the time we went to closing. They also wanted to change the contract to keep some of the major fixtures in the house. We were on a tight schedule and didn't have a lot of room for error. Hopefully we could work everything out, and soon.

We started researching the house we were buying; after all, it was the Eastern Regional Headquarters for the Hari Krishna's. We thought it would be wise to see what that might entail. We came across the web-site for the Hari Krishna's living at the house. The web-site listed "our" house as the world headquarters. It also invited everyone to come by on any Sunday for a free meal. We started to wonder who would be stopping by for dinner. So, we asked for a slight modification of the sales contract to include a clause requiring the sellers to modify their web-site on or before the closing date. We didn't want to be "rude," but we had enough to do without cooking dinner for a bunch of people we didn't know.

Then we hit a small snag with the people who had rented our condo. The nice professional couple, who had good credit and were planning to get married in May, were no longer a couple. She caught him with another woman and apparently that wasn't exactly what she was looking for in a marriage. Fortunately for us, he still wanted to rent the condo. She wanted him tarred and feathered, among other things. We stayed out of their personal lives and were just happy we still had a renter.

We were now eleven days from making the two biggest financial transactions of our lives. We thought the sale of the townhouse would go smoothly, although our realtor felt the buying realtor was falling down on the job. She said "don't worry; I'll pick up the slack." Easy for her to say, we were worriers by nature.

Meanwhile back at the condo we were making progress on the packing and cleaning. The animals seemed to be taking things rather well. The one exception was Momma Kitty who was still guarding us from the "Under the Bed Monsters." She felt her presence was required twenty-four hours a day at this post. She was so stressed by the happenings she wouldn't even come out from under the bed to use the litter box.

That was very evident at 2 a.m. one morning when she produced a rather large specimen under the bed. It produced enough of an odor to wake Bob and me from a sound sleep. At first I was going to blame Bob, but I knew he was pretty well house broken by now. The next likely suspect had to be Boomer (we didn't think there was any way a cat could produce something that BIG)!!!

While inspecting the stool sample, we found traces of blood. This earned Boomer a trip to the vet for a rather embarrassing prostate exam. Everything tested out fine. The vet told us to keep an eye on him and watch for any additional bloody stool.

Then we discovered Boomer wasn't at fault. The next day Momma Kitty, who we now called Momma Mia because of her fondness for Italian dishes, left another deposit under the bed right in front of us.

The stress of the move was freaking her out so much that she was doing everything possible to avoid coming out from under the bed. We fixed the problem by setting her up with a private litter box under the bed. We always found it was easier to adapt to the animals rather than the other way around. After that everything was okay, but she never did apologize to Boomer for the unnecessary prostate exam.

Adventures in Moving

It was official!!! We were moving to our new and, hopefully, permanent location. We had everything planned and scheduled in nifty computer spreadsheets. Our schedule was laid out with plenty of room for most contingencies. Or so we thought.

Unfortunately, the old saying about best laid plans reared its ugly head. We did survive, but it was one of those times in life that was only funny when you looked back on it. This was how it went.

Thursday, April 22: Left work on time, amid a chorus of "Good Lucks," with Bob and me saying we WILL see you Saturday, right (for those coworkers who agreed to help us move)?

We were all excited about the move and the beginning of our new life working with animals. Nothing could go wrong.

Then we got a call from our realtor; the realtor for the people buying our townhouse was too busy doing "realtor stuff" to do the termite inspection. Our realtor could set it up, but couldn't let the inspector in; could we cover it? Minor thing, hopefully everything else would go as planned.

Friday, April 23: We picked up the food and beer for Saturday and finished all of the packing before 7 p.m. We were ahead of schedule!!! No fur-balls or any other accidents on the carpet at the condo!!! Life was good!

Saturday, April 24: It was a bright and sunny day, a good day for moving furniture. We loaded up the food and beer in the car and picked up our twenty-eight foot Ryder truck at 8 a.m. We arrived at the townhouse and had the truck backed up in the driveway by 8:30. Oops, the next door neighbor was blocked in and needed to get out. Okay, the truck was in position by 8:37. Bob and I started loading the truck. Oops, we forgot blankets to protect the furniture and ropes to secure everything. Okay, a quick call to Bob's mom to bring blankets and I went to the hardware store for ropes and stuff.

By the time our helpers arrived we had a very efficient set up: Bob and his sister Diane were in the truck stacking and packing while the rest of us alternated bringing boxes and furniture to the truck. The loading proceeded with relatively minor incidents: At one point Diane got packed behind the kitchen table, but with a little reloading we managed to free her. We could have just left her there, but Bob didn't think she wanted to spend five days in the back of the truck, and we did have more loading to do.

Around 11:30 we realized we had a problem. We only had about four feet of room left on the truck, and we had at least nine feet of stuff to load, plus we still had all the stuff from the condo and Diane's house. We put a few of the more critical items on the truck and reluctantly put everything else in the garage.

We fed everyone and then headed for the condo to load whatever would fit on the back of the truck. We thought we should at least load the heavy stuff while we had help, so we loaded the couch and a few boxes, thanked everyone profusely and parked the truck. Hey, at least the house, the furniture and the people all survived.

Sunday, April 25: We had to borrow a cargo van a day early to finish getting our stuff out of the townhouse we were selling. Getting a flat tire on the van put us a little behind schedule, but not too bad. Then we were off to Bob's father's birthday celebration.

Good News! The settlement time on the townhouse we were selling was moved from 2 p.m. to 10 a.m. on Tuesday! That gave us a few more hours of breathing room between the settlement times on the two houses.

Monday, April 26: We drained the fish pond and managed to catch all the fish (fortunately, no one witnessed the sacred fish catching dance, or heard the words of wisdom uttered when I wiped out and landed on my butt in the middle of the pond).

By 5 p.m. we had sloshed the fish into the van that would be their home for the next forty-eight hours. We barely had time to feed the critters, shower and head to the new house for the walk through.

The walk through went okay. The whole house needed extensive cleaning, but that was okay, we had cleaning people lined up. The grass hadn't been cut at all that year, but the owner said it was to be cut the next day. The carpet hadn't been cleaned, but the carpet cleaners were scheduled for later that night. We were starting to see a trend. Minor things we thought, but still more details to worry about.

In the meantime, the walk through for the townhouse was taking place. The townhouse was empty so we figured all had gone well. As it turned out, the realtor and her clients had some "major" issues with the townhouse. They called with "grave" concerns about the closet wall; there were two "holes" where we removed the removable hanging bar. She accused us of "concealing major damage." Our response was "huh????"

Tuesday, April 27: The time had arrived!!! This was the day Bob and I would complete two of the biggest financial transactions of our lives. To start, we had to repair the two "holes" (small indentations from the removable bar) in the closet at the townhouse. No big deal; we'd do that on the way to meet our realtor for settlement on the new house.

But first we had to settle on the townhouse. To say the settlement company was inconvenient was an understatement. The selling realtor picked the company and insisted the closing had to be done there. Everyone else had to drive at least forty minutes, but at least it was convenient to her. Once we arrived we noticed it was also in one of the more dangerous areas of D.C. Even the churches had bars over the doors and windows.

Our realtor reluctantly said good-bye to her Lexus, and we were "buzzed" into the settlement company's office. The receptionist informed us that our settlement date had been moved to 10 a.m. on Wednesday by the other realtor. Apparently she forgot to call to inform us of this minor change. We really didn't want to return so our realtor asked if we could sign the paperwork, get our checks and get out of this "*&!!@#" place? No, the other realtor had the paperwork and she had more pressing matters. Fortunately, we didn't need the proceeds from the townhouse to go to closing on the other house.

We would have to do some rearranging and return the next day to close on the townhouse. Fortunately, the townhouse was titled in my name so Bob wouldn't need to be at the closing. He would be free to cover the rest of the stuff we had planned for the next day.

Now it was time to buy the new house. The settlement was at 4 p.m. Bob and I arrived at 3:50 and were the only ones there. That gave us some cause for concern, especially considering the events of that morning. We figured what were the odds of getting skunked twice in one day?

Our realtor showed up at 4:05, still ranting about the morning events or lack thereof. At 4:15 the selling realtor called: She had locked all of her keys in her car and would not be able make it to closing. Could our realtor pick up her commission check and drop it off?

We were still missing another key party, the people who were selling us the house. At 4:30 they called: Their son injured himself at a convenience store and they had to stop at the emergency room before they could make it to closing. Things weren't looking good at all.

Eventually the sellers showed up and the process started. Then we had another small problem: Even though we didn't need the proceeds from the sale of the townhouse for closing, we had to prove we sold the townhouse and were rid of the mortgage payment before they would approve the loan for the new house. That wouldn't be a problem; we were going to settlement the next day. The title company would hold our papers until then.

Finally the papers were signed, the T's crossed, the I's dotted, and the keys to our new house turned over to us. The title company gave us a bottle of champagne and sent us on our way.

Now the fun began; we had to unload the fish and the twenty-eight foot truck so we could reload it with the contents of the condo the next day.

Wednesday, April 28: Today was the day Bob and I really moved into "our" new house. All of our stuff would finally be in one place. The cleaning people were scheduled for 9 a.m. My father would arrive around the same time to see the house and supervise the cleaners. Then there was the small detail of going to settlement on the townhouse, but that would be over by 1:00 p.m.

Now here's what really happened on that "special" day:

7 a.m.: Bob and I woke up. None of the animals had peed, pooped or puked in the condo. Life was good.

8 a.m.: My father arrived at the condo and we loaded his minivan.

8:15 a.m.: We loaded my car.

8:30 a.m.: We started loading the rental truck; things were still going well.

8:45 a.m.: My father and I set off for the new house. Bob would finish loading the truck.

9:15 a.m.: We arrived at the new house. The cleaning people were supposed to be here at 9 a.m. but they weren't. Maybe they got caught in the same traffic we did.

9:25 a.m.: My father fell down the stairs. He didn't want me to call an ambulance, but I could tell his shoulder was hurting. It must have been the macho factor from his World War II Navy days. He just wouldn't admit he had hurt himself. I couldn't call for an ambulance anyway; we wouldn't have phone service until the following day and Bob had both cell phones.

9:40 a.m.: Bob arrived with the rental truck ready to start unloading furniture. He took one look at my father's ashen face and asked what happened. My dad said his shoulder hurt a little, but should be okay in a little while. Bob was persistent and did his "I always wanted to be a paramedic routine." After one look at the shoulder, he used his cell phone to find a doctor for my father.

9:55 a.m.: The cleaning people finally arrived one hour late. We told them to go ahead and start cleaning. I left to close on the townhouse while Bob took my father to the doctor. We had already called Bob's mom to supervise the cleaning people.

10:10 a.m.: I arrived at the settlement company's office. I was told to go home. The settlement was off. The other realtor didn't like the look of the sprinkler system in the townhouse. Apparently she had no concept that all these things were to be done prior to settlement; all I could say was "what a moron!!!" The other realtor would not return our realtor's phone calls. I threw a tirade about putting the townhouse back on the market. We called the other realtor leaving a message that the deal was off. It was amazing how fast the other realtor called to tell us things were okay, and please don't cancel the contract. It was all just a small misunderstanding. Settlement was rescheduled for 4 p.m. on Thursday.

11:30 a.m.: The cleaning people claimed to be finished. I couldn't tell if they had actually cleaned anything.

11:45 a.m.: Bob called. They had the results from the doctor; my father had broken his shoulder in several places. He had an appointment with an orthopedic specialist later in the day.

2:10 p.m.: Time to leave for my father's appointment with the orthopedic doctor. We decided to take my father's minivan to the doctor. I hopped in, put the key in the ignition and turned the key, but nothing happened. My father had left the lights on and the battery was deader than the proverbial doornail. We moved my father into the Camero, one of our two-seater cars. Trust me; it was very difficult to get a seventy-five year old man, with a broken shoulder, into a Camero.

After we left, Bob headed back to the condo with the rental truck to meet a couple of helpers and finish loading the furniture. I wasn't sure what happened at the condo, but I was told a lot of sweating and grunting was involved and Bob wasn't smiling or smoking a cigarette afterwards.

2:35 p.m.: My father and I got lost in Annapolis and ended up at the Naval Academy football field. It wasn't all that bad; at least some of the football players were cute.

3:00 p.m.: We found the doctor's office.

3:15 p.m.: My father and I saw the doctor. He asked for the X-rays and I said "what X-rays?" Oh yeah, we left them in the minivan. We took more X-rays.

3:30 p.m.: The doctor looked at my father's new X-rays. He said "oh my." I was thinking it wasn't good when the specialist used a phrase like that. Final diagnosis: my father had crushed his shoulder joint. It would need to be replaced. The doctor's staff would schedule the surgery for the next week. We should come back Friday for an EKG and pre-op blood tests. Then we were given several prescriptions for pain killers. I was a little disappointed to find out they were all for my father. It turned out he would also be our first house guest for the next few months. There was no way he could take care of himself alone at his house.

4:30 p.m.: It was time to move the critters (originally we thought this would be the most difficult part of the move). Once again we stuffed the Rude Cats into their respective carriers and settled in for a serenaded ride back to the new house.

The house was huge. The cats would be exploring for hours. There was a master bedroom suite along with three other bedrooms on the top floor. The main floor had two living rooms, an office space, an eat-in kitchen and a large dining room, not to mention a full bath. The basement had the "temple room" and two more rooms that were nicely finished and overlooked the back yard.

The House that Became a Sanctuary

5:45 p.m.: We arrived at the house and took all the cats (still in their carriers) into the "cat room" (formerly the temple room) and released them. Abbey and Momma Mia immediately crawled into a window and huddled there, looking pathetic. Cali, insulted she had to be in a carrier to begin with, set off on an adventure to explore the house. Tia wasn't far behind.

6:35 p.m.: Momma Mia discovered a small entryway that led her to the wonderful world between the floors of the house. She eventually came out of the tunnel over the furnace area and managed to turn the furnace switch off when she jumped down.

7:15 p.m.: We were still trying to figure out why the furnace wouldn't work.

7:25 p.m.: How the hell did the furnace get turned off?

8:30 p.m.: We resigned ourselves to the fact we would not get anything else accomplished that day. We set up the sleeper sofa for my father and threw a mattress down on the floor for Bob and me. Boomer promptly peed on the mattress. That was the perfect ending to a "perfect" day.

Thursday, April 29: After making sure my father was whacked up on Percoset, Bob and I headed to the condo to finish the cleaning. We ran the dishwasher one last time to make sure it worked. On Friday we would order a new dishwasher for the condo.

3 p.m.: I met our realtor to head back into Washington D.C. to deal with our final problem: selling the townhouse. This time we made it through the settlement and escaped with check in hand, and hopefully no returns to the settlement office.

Now we had to fight through rush hour traffic to make it back to Crofton in time to wrap up the loan on the new house. Then it was off to meet the new renter at the condo, explain the dishwasher problem and turn the keys over to him.

Friday, April 30: It was our fifth wedding anniversary!!! We were celebrating it by getting EKG's and blood work for my father's surgery, ordering a dishwasher for the condo, trying to fit the couch into the living room, and taking my father to his house to pick up more clothes.

As long as we were in the neighborhood, we borrowed my father's riding lawn mower to cut the hay field that was our lawn. The lawn guy the previous owner said was coming to mow the lawn never showed up. Unfortunately, the battery on the lawn mower was in pretty much the same shape as the battery in the minivan, dead as a doornail.

So that was how our move went. We spent our time arranging and rearranging the furniture, preparing for my father's surgery (and extended visit) and getting ready for the onslaught of kitten season.

We also realized our transportation situation had changed and driving two small sports cars wasn't going to work anymore. We reluctantly grew up a little and traded our Camero in for a four wheel drive Chevy Suburban.

Judging from the way this week went, Bob and I figured we would be ready to move again soon, in like twenty years!!!

Goldie & Bones Arrive

Now that we had survived the move to our new house (although barely), it was time for the daunting task of placing furniture and unpacking the thousands of boxes crammed with all our stuff (okay, maybe only a hundred boxes). We managed to find most of the important stuff, but several vital household items, such as the TV remote control, were still missing in action. Bob had to return to the caveman method of changing channels and throw something at the TV until it hit a channel he liked.

A few weeks later Bob and I were back to volunteering at Save A Life and occasionally working at Uncle Nicky's. It was during one of our days at Save A Life that we decided to bring Goldie home from the shelter. He'd been there for a long time now trying to find a home and just wasn't having any luck. We now had this big house and felt it was time to reunite Goldie with his mom.

Goldie seemed quite pleased with the idea of returning home with us. Until now, this cat would run and hide every time a kitty carrier was brought within six feet of him. This time he went right into the carrier without any fuss.

We made the trip back home and set Goldie free in the living room. We were curious to see if his old buddies would remember him, especially his mom. We would have to wait a little while to see how he did with the rest of the cats. He was a little freaked out with all the changes since he lived with us in the townhouse. He went straight up to the top of the kitchen cabinets. At least we could see him.

It was about this time Bob started having what I called "lawn disasters." Our new house had about two acres of lawn. Obviously, the lawn would grow and periodically needed to be cut. I decided this was a Bob job. He agreed to this arrangement, but would need a riding lawn mower to do the job properly (or at least that's what he told me).

The first time he mowed the lawn he used my father's riding lawn mower. It probably would have worked much better if he hadn't run over some discarded bicycle shorts that had been thrown in the yard. Spandex can really wrap tightly around mower blades. (We didn't want to think about it too much, but if the bicyclist left his spandex in the yard, what did he wear for the trip home?) Luckily Bob was willing to lift the mower up while I crawled underneath it and cut the fabric away from the blades. About halfway through the process I started wondering if I had done anything to tick Bob off recently; after all, he was holding a lawn mower directly over my head. If I had done anything, it must not have been all that bad; Bob didn't drop the mower until after I was done.

There was another lawn mower incident shortly after we purchased a brand spanking new lawn mower. Bob managed to get the tarp covering the temporary fish pond tangled up in the mower blades. We had to repeat the process performed during the spandex incident. I soon resigned myself to the fact that when Bob went out to mow the lawn, I should be ready with a pair of scissors.

With all the lawn mower incidents, we also had some concerns that our new neighbors were watching us wondering what kind of morons had moved in next door. We didn't realize we had another pair of eyes watching us from the woods. Those eyes belonged to a beautiful, but intimidating looking dog. He made himself known to us one afternoon while Bob and I were walking through our backyard. All of a sudden, a big furry creature was standing behind Bob, wagging its tail. At first I couldn't decide if it was a bear or a horse. It was a really big, fortunately friendly, dog. He stopped by for an ear scritch and then went on his way.

The next time we met the big dog, Boomer was with us. The big dog immediately went to Boomer and started playing. Boomer seemed to like the big dog, but really had no interest in the playing ritual. For all his bravado, Boomer was no match for this 100 pound puppy.

We learned from one of our neighbors that this big guy didn't have a home. He had been abandoned and sort of became the neighborhood stray. They hinted that maybe we could take him in as a buddy for Boomer? We were starting to get attached to the big guy and worried about him when he didn't show up for his nightly visits.

By now Abbey and Blackie were our only foster cats. They were doing okay in our house, but they really needed a home where they could have undivided attention. Fortunately, such a home seemed right around the corner. A family was coming by to meet the girls that weekend. Bob and I had the foresight to lock them in a room before the family arrived. After all, we didn't need the cats pulling an "Alien Transportation Maneuver" and disappearing just when we needed them.

The visit didn't start well. Upon entering the house, the six year old daughter saw Boomer and immediately let out an ear-piercing shriek. At that point most of the cats took off for parts unknown. When the little girl saw all the furry bodies running through the house, she let out another ear-piercing shriek. This time Bob and I headed for the aspirin. The family finally made it into the room with Abbey and Blackie. Unfortunately, every time one of the cats brushed up against the little girl she screamed. This certainly wasn't going well. We hadn't given up yet, but we were slowly losing our optimism.

Bob and I were exchanging looks wondering what we had gotten ourselves into. How could we coerce the family into leaving before either the cats or the little girl had a nervous breakdown? Just when we thought all hope was lost, the little girl calmed down and started petting the cats. She immediately thought that was cool. The cats were rubbing up against her and were purring. I guess the cats weren't all that scary; the cats came to the same conclusion about her. The family just couldn't separate the two siblings and adopted them both. Success!

After that things were quiet for a couple of weeks until I got a call from the lady who had adopted Brownie the previous summer. There was a kitten living in a storm drain on a school parking lot. It had been there for about three weeks. Some kids were feeding it, but with all the traffic around the parking lot, the kitten was sure to be run over. Could we help?

Armed with kitty toys, food, gloves, a trap and good intentions we headed to the storm drain. Sure enough, there was a kitten in the drain. That was the easy part. Now all we had to do was coax it out of the drain and into the trap. We set everything up, baited the trap, and waited for the kitten. Eventually, the kitten peeked out of the storm drain to see if the coast was clear. He saw the tasty treats leading up to the trap. He was falling for the old trail of food into the trap trick. We thought we had him, and then the school bus arrived to pick up the kids. Realizing he now had an audience, the kitten went down the drain along with our hopes to easily catch him.

Our kitten-catching setup was starting to attract attention from the kids and parents going in and out of the school. Everyone was looking to Bob and me as the experts and expected us to immediately capture the kitten. Unfortunately, with a big audience, it would be much tougher to coax this little guy into the trap. We asked the people to go about their business and we'd let them know how things went. Nobody would listen. We took the initiative and left, hoping that like the pied piper, everyone would follow us and leave the kitten alone.

When we went back to the parking lot a little later we found the kitten playing around the trap. He was pulling the "bait" out of the trap without tripping the mechanism. Okay, so it was a smart kitten.

Bob then took a different approach to capturing the kitten and tried to make friends with the little guy. He wandered over and sat on the curb close to where the kitten was playing. The kitten eventually eased over to Bob and started rubbing all over his shoes, but drew the line at letting Bob touch him. Every time Bob made a move toward the kitten, he scurried a few feet away.

It was starting to get late, and people were beginning to show up with their dogs. We found out the school yard was also the local dog walking area. People passing by were starting to give us some really strange "I'm calling the cops" kind of looks. Hey, it wasn't every day you see two people sitting on the ground by a storm drain with assorted animal capture paraphernalia around them.

We caught a break when someone walked their dog past Bob and the kitten. The kitten was distracted long enough for Bob to scruff it, me to open the carrier, and Bob to put the wiggly kitten in it. A confused kitten ended up safely in the carrier wondering what had just happened. We named him Mack; he just had a Mack look about him.

Mack's abrupt capture didn't seem to affect his sweetness at all. By the end of the night he was grooming Bob's beard and rolling over for tummy rubs. It was a weird phenomenon, but kittens always seemed drawn to Bob's beard. I guess they thought he was their mom (or, maybe Bob just had something good in his beard left over from breakfast).

The following Saturday Mack made the trip to the Save A Life shelter for his initial vet work. He was a big hit at the shelter. He was such a suck up that everyone wanted to hold him. He even climbed up Bill, one of the shelter owners, and started grooming his beard. I guess he wasn't exclusive to Bob, and any guy with a beard would do.

This particular Saturday was a special day for one of the other residents at the shelter; it was the day the shelter mascot, Bones, retired. You see Bones was pretty much a fixture at the shelter. Being Bill's favorite cat, he had special privileges. While Bones lived at the shelter it was understood that under no circumstances was he to be adopted to anyone.

That all changed after nine years as their mascot. Bill and Janice wanted Bones to live in a real home. They asked us if we would take him. We were honored they felt we were good enough for Bones and immediately said yes.

Bones, the Newest Rude Cat

Bones was pretty much unflappable after spending most of his life at the shelter. He was accustomed to seeing cats loaded into kitty carriers and never coming back. He wasn't used to being loaded into a carrier himself. He certainly wasn't used to being put in a car. On the way home he was meowing so intently that little Mack started trying to reach into the carrier to comfort him.

Bones' first few hours at our house were something of a riot. You could almost see the wheels turning in his head: Litter box: check. Food: check. Water: okay. Another cat: it's Goldie! I remember you! Cool. Eventually, Bones made his way upstairs and met the other cats.

Tia, still the queen, explained the rules to him. He understood. Then he saw himself in the mirror. He just couldn't understand why this cat was staring back at him. Then Cali, our resident brat, arrived to check him out. Bones, who was still following proper cat protocol, tried to introduce himself. Cali, who believed the universe should revolve around her, didn't follow such protocols! She bopped him a good one on the ears. The rest of the night went pretty smoothly and Bones had no problem adapting to the other cats or sleeping in bed with humans.

The Population Explosion

It was hard to believe, but after six months we still hadn't finished unpacking some of the boxes from the move. At this point if there was something we couldn't find, we either went through the boxes, or gave up and bought another one. One day we'd finish unpacking, but we weren't holding our breath.

Then we got a call from Tina, one of Bob's coworkers at the Census Bureau. There was a litter of kittens living at a Taco Bell in southern Maryland. Could we help her catch them? Even though we weren't ready to go full bore with the animal rescue yet, we didn't feel right saying no, especially if someone else was willing to trap them. Yes, we'd help out. We just had to supply the traps and the carriers. It sounded like a good deal to us, so we loaded up the traps, carriers, food most cats couldn't resist, and instructions for catching "wild" kittens and off we went.

As it turned out, Tina did things a little differently than we suggested; she used the instructions for catching wild kittens as padding in the bottom of the carriers. She skipped the food we provided and baited the carriers with what the kittens had been living on in the dumpster: soft taco supremes. When the kitten went into the carrier for the taco, she just closed the door behind it. Not our normal bait and trap procedure, but hey, it worked. At least it worked on the first two kittens. She caught the third kitten using the trap. At least the traps weren't a total waste. In the end Tina caught three, thirteen week old kittens.

We made the trip to Tina's house to pick up the three little kittens. It was easy getting them into the car; Tina already had them in a cage that would easily fit into the backseat. Handling the "Taco Bell" kittens once we got home was another matter altogether. We were spoiled by the beginner's luck we had with our first experiences with feral kittens. Two of the Taco Bell kittens were truly feral; much more so than Cali, Abbey, or Blackie were. They were even more feral than Momma Mia's litter of kittens from two years ago. For some reason the third kitten was tame. She wanted to be picked up and loved all the attention from us humans. She was easy to deal with and was adopted a few weeks later at a Friskies sponsored cat show in Baltimore.

The other two kittens, Penty and Gunny, were another matter altogether. They bit us, Hard! They hissed! They spit at us! Then we had another problem: They had to be moved.

We were keeping the Taco Bell kittens quarantined in the basement bathroom. We now needed that room for a mother cat and her six kittens we agreed to take in. Penty and Gunny had to move to a cage in the office. We just had to catch them first.

Somehow I managed to draw the short straw. I was assigned to catch the kittens and move them, while Bob went to pick up the new mommy and her kittens. I got ready. I took two carriers. I brought gloves. I had the cage upstairs in the office ready. I caught the kittens and stuffed them in the carrier. The gloves were toast, but at least I had the kittens. Penty and Gunny weren't too happy. When they got out of the cage and hid behind the desk three hours later, I wasn't happy either.

Bob arrived with the mother cat, AC, and her six kittens a little later in the day. They were all very playful and incredibly sweet. AC's story was pretty common: "I really meant to get her fixed, but she went into heat and slipped out the door." Now the people didn't want her or the kittens.

AC and Her Kittens Doing the "Drive-By Eating" Thing

It took two days before AC's kittens, Duncan, Amanda, Fitz, Connor, Tessa and Ebony, got bored with the bathroom and started breaking out to explore the rest of the basement (we were on a *Highlander* TV series kick at this point and named most of the litter after characters on the show). The reaction by the rest of the Rude Cats was interesting. Bones came around the corner, saw the kittens and hit the brakes so hard he almost left skid marks. Then he remembered he was neutered and felt relieved (they couldn't be his). He decided AC needed some help and started grooming and litter box training the kittens. After all, he was a sensitive male.

Boomer's reaction to the kittens was hilarious. At first he seemed happy we finally had something smaller than him. Then he started trying to keep track of the kittens as they darted about. For awhile we thought he was going to have a nervous breakdown. The kittens just wouldn't hold still long enough for him to count properly.

Boomer Supervising AC's Kittens

By this time we were up to a total of nineteen cats and one dog in the house. We also had the "Big Dog" outside that several neighbors were still asking us to make dog number two. So, we were especially grateful when all of AC's kittens were ready to attend the cat show at the end of September. We had a huge success at the show with all but little Fitz finding homes. AC herself did not go to the show. She was recovering from raising a large family and still needed her dreaded spay surgery.

We felt bad that little Fitz was the only kitten left, but it didn't seem to have him all that worried. He soon started looking for new playmates. Penty and Gunny were more interested in hissing at Bob and me than playing, so they were out. Then Jasmin arrived.

Jasmin was dropped off at the Save A Life shelter by a tearful couple who "just couldn't keep her." Although terrified, she seemed pretty friendly, so feeling sorry for her, we brought her home. She started out quarantined in one of the upstairs bedrooms. That arrangement didn't last long as Jasmin was way too active to be by herself. Her first visitor was a somewhat bored Fitz (who was about half her size). He tackled her head-on and a somewhat surprised Jasmin ended up flat on her back looking up at Fitz. Not to be outdone, Jasmin immediately took off after Fitz. The chase was on for roughly twenty-two hours a day.

Fortunately, Fitz soon found a home with a husband and wife lawyer team from Virginia. At least if Fitz got into trouble, he'd have plenty of free legal counsel.

Then Jasmin, our tuxedo clad, high energy foster kitten and AC found a new home together. Jasmin went with the warning she was a high energy kitten. Don't leave any breakables you care about out in the open. AC didn't need any warnings; she was a well behaved retired mom, just looking for a lap to sit on.

Things at the house were starting to quiet down again, meaning only one thing: we got a call from a lady in Laurel, Maryland who was trapping cats and kittens in a feral colony. Could we help?

Working with our usual forethought and organization, we told the lady yes, we could take several kittens. Go ahead and start bringing them in and we'd work at socializing them and finding them new homes. Then we started thinking (not always our strong suit). She was bringing upwards of six kittens. Feral kittens. The kittens would have to be in cages. We took inventory. We had one cage and Penty and Gunny were in it. We made a hurried call to our wholesale supplier. All they had were ferret cages. Close enough. We even managed to get the cages put together before the first two kittens arrived.

The first arrivals were a brother and sister, about four months old. They were promptly named Scully and Mulder (I was into the *X-Files* at that point). Then Coally and Fraidi arrived a few days later. Our office was starting to get a little crowded with all the cages filled with kittens.

The Rude Cats weren't too pleased with these developments. After all, the new cats were getting more attention than they were. They started getting even in several ways: hairballs started showing up in shoes, clothes, and on the TV remote (that one really hurt Bob). The next development really turned their lives around.

Remember the Big Dog that was kind of the neighborhood stray? Well, he was still hanging out in our back yard. He was a really nice dog and still didn't appear to have a home. Bob and I kept trying to talk ourselves out of taking him in, until we saw him almost hit by a car. Bob commented that wrestling with him in the yard was a lot of fun. Little eight pound Boomer just couldn't provide enough of a challenge for Bob.

Okay, we were getting attached to him and were beginning to lose sleep worrying about him. We even had kind of picked out a name for him: Bruno.

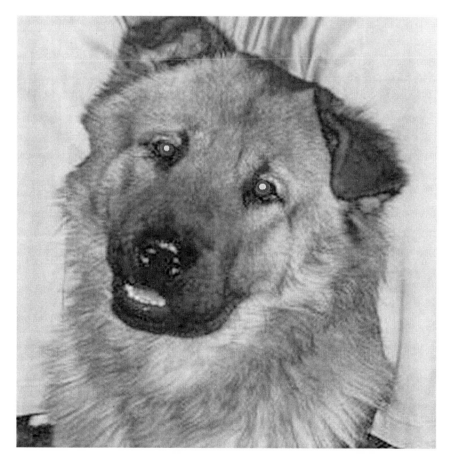

The "Big Dog," Bruno

The decision was made for us when Hurricane Floyd passed through the area. We saw the Big Dog out in the yard as the storm started, so we put him in the garage. His first night did not go all that well. He had never been confined before and kind of panicked. He tried to dig his way out through the garage door. Since our garage door was insulated with Styrofoam, it looked like a snowman had exploded when we opened the door the next morning. After that, we knew we were "done for" and Bruno became our second dog.

The next step was to introduce Bruno to the cats. Our initial attempts were far from successful. The cats felt Boomer was no threat and got along well with him. Bruno was another story. To the cats he was a 100 pound, drooling fur-ball looking for a party. To Bruno the cats were self-energizing interactive dog toys. Whenever Bruno would see a cat, he would run towards it to make friends (at least that was what we were hoping he was doing). The cat would take off for parts unknown somewhere on the third floor. In an effort to accelerate the process of integrating Bruno with the cats, we constructed a barrier to the third floor. That would give the cats a safe place to escape (or so we thought)! Bob had to reevaluate the materials he used for the barrier; it only slowed Bruno down by about two seconds.

Obviously, Bruno was going to take some work before he fit into our mainly feline household. He had survived for several years utilizing his excellent hunting skills. It would be a challenge to convince him the cats were part of his pack and not tasty appetizers. They couldn't all be easy like Boomer.

The next week it was time for Bruno to make a visit to Dr. Richman. He was loaded into the Suburban, and it was off to the clinic. I guess we hadn't given Dr. Richman all the details about Bruno, just that he was a dog. That earned us a lecture on how difficult a neuter surgery can be on mature large dogs, especially those of Bruno's breeding (he did have a distinctive Chow look). After the lecture, Dr. Richman pointed out several scars on his body courtesy of Chows that came out of anesthesia in a bad mood. Hopefully Bruno wouldn't add to his collection.

Dr. Richman went ahead with the surgery, but had an emergency syringe loaded with knock out juice ready to go in one of Bruno's veins. He wasn't taking any chances. If Bruno started to wake up, he was taking a quick trip back to "la la land." Fortunately, Bruno woke up his usual happy-go-lucky self; he was just a little lighter. He spent most of the next day trying to figure out what was different. Something just seemed to be missing.

Then we received a call from the caregiver of the Laurel colony. Another cat was on its way. One problem: all our cages were full. We decided Mulder and Scully were tame enough to have the run of their room. They seemed more than agreeable with the plan and graciously turned their cage over to the new cat, Taz.

By now we had a bunch of new cats and it was time to have them all spayed and neutered. We were off to see Dr. Richman for another round of surgeries, vaccinations and blood work. It went well for most of the cats, except Taz (her name was short for Tasmanian Devil, and we soon found out why). Bob was holding her for the vet to inject the knock out shot, when Taz took one look at the needle and pretty much said "NO WAY," curled her body around Bob's arm, pushed off and started a twenty minute chase around the building. Dr. Richman calmly sedated the next cat and said he would get back to her later. At least Bob didn't drip too much blood during the chase around the clinic.

By now it was getting close to Christmas, which usually meant Christmas decorations and Christmas trees. Bob and I thought about the tradition of putting up the tree and reminiscing about the different ornaments as they were carefully hung on the branches. Then we took stock of our environment: nine cats, most of whom viewed Christmas ornaments as an integral part of their kitty soccer games, one Min Pin, and one large dog that had trouble stopping when running full tilt. Plus we still hadn't located the Christmas decorations since the move. We skipped the tree that year. We just put reindeer antlers on Bruno.

Y2K and the Stray Dog

By now fall was passing into the winter holidays and the potential disasters of the dreaded "Y2K" computer glitches were upon us. For many it was an exciting adventure into a new century. For Bob and me it meant years of planning, rewriting code and testing applications to ensure the computer world at the Census Bureau wouldn't come crashing to a halt. New Year's Day came and went. All went well with the computers and now we could get back to focusing on what really mattered to us, the animals.

In early January we ran into a problem with one of our adoptions. One of the cats we placed into a new home wasn't working out. AC and Jasmin were adopted together, but where Jasmin fit right into the new household, AC was having problems getting along with their other cat. She started displaying her displeasure by urinating all over their house. Her family finally gave up and reluctantly returned AC to us. They would still really like another cat to play with Jasmin though.

By now, Gunny was tame enough to be certified as lap fungus. Since it seemed like a really good home we did an "exchange" of AC for Gunny. Although she was very nervous at first, Gunny settled into her new home with Jasmin and her older brother Saber. They were the perfect match. Now we just had to put AC into our behavior modification program and get her ready for a new home.

Then we got a call from one of our neighbors. There was a stray dog "living" on the side of the road about a mile from our house. The dog had been "dumped" with a big pile of trash and was waiting patiently for her family to return. She would only leave the pile of trash when someone tried to approach her. Then she would run into the woods and disappear until the coast was clear.

Bob thought this was something he had to tackle. So off we went in the Suburban. I was told to hang out in the car and stay as quiet as possible (normally I wouldn't let Bob talk to me that way, but he seemed to have a plan).

The long process of rescuing this beautiful white German Shepherd began. Bob took his dog treats and sat on the ground about twenty feet from the pile of trash. The dog would take a treat and then back away showing her teeth and growling the whole time. Bob would make a little progress at winning the dog over and then one of our neighbors would stop by to see if we had caught the dog yet. At one point this little stretch of road seemed busier than Grand Central Station. Whenever someone stopped by to check on our status, Bob would have to start all over again with the dog. This went on for about two hours.

Finally it was late enough that people quit stopping by. Bob made a breakthrough when the dog ran into the woods and returned, dropping the remains of a rabbit in Bob's lap. I got the distinct impression Bob wasn't all that thrilled with the gift, but appreciated the thought. Finally she came over and put her head in Bob's lap. The rest was easy. He slipped a lead over her head and led her over to the Suburban.

The dog, who we named Sheba, turned out to be a young, sweet girl. Unfortunately, we were not set up to take in dogs. We called a fellow rescuer who was happy to take Sheba once we described her. In a stroke of luck, her mother was looking for a dog just like her. We drove Sheba to her new home and let out a sigh of relief that things worked out so well. All the neighbors were grateful the dog was no longer hanging out on the side of the road too.

What's in a Name?

By now it was obvious that working with animals had become more than a hobby for us. It was during a January blizzard that Bob and I took the plunge and started our own non-profit, no-kill animal sanctuary. Most people cleaned their houses or surfed the internet when they were snowed in; we began the paperwork to incorporate our organization and become an IRS approved charity. We wanted to make sure we accomplished something worthwhile during the "blizzard."

A lot of people wondered why we chose the name Rude Ranch Animal Rescue. For this, we must give credit to Dr. Robert Harrison, owner of the Belair Veterinary Hospital. He was the vet who had taken care of our personal pets for many years. When we first started rescuing animals, we didn't have a firm game plan for the veterinary care. Truth be told, we didn't have any plan at all. We started out using Dr. Richman at the Save A Life shelter. He was great, but he was forty-five minutes away. It was really eating into our vacation time running the animals back and forth.

One day Dr. Harrison asked us if we ever needed veterinary help with the animals we were rescuing. We said "you bet" and entered into a new agreement for vet care with Dr. Harrison and his staff. He wanted to give us a price break for the rescued animals, but needed to create a method to track this separate from our personal pets. Easy problem to fix; he'd just set up a new account for the rescued animals. He decided that Rude Ranch sounded good. We had a lot of animals at our house and our last name was Rude. We agreed that it made sense, and from that point forward, we officially became known as Rude Ranch. When we became a full fledged charity, we thought the name would work. Yes it was different, but at least people would probably remember it. We made a slight modification and made it Rude Ranch Animal Rescue and the rest was history.

Dr. Harrison with One of His Surgical Patients

Now that we were an official charity, we had to start thinking about an image that would represent Rude Ranch. Our new buddy Bones was a big ham and loved to pose for the camera. He had a regal way of wrapping his tail around his body and had a look that melted hearts. That was it; Bones started his new career as the official mascot of our new animal sanctuary. We even had a graphic artist use his image to design the Rude Ranch logo. Bones would forever be the face of Rude Ranch.

Then it was time to make another huge life decision. In six months Bob would resign from the Census Bureau and concentrate on helping animals full-time. The animal rescue business was getting busier and busier. We just couldn't keep up with the demand and hold down full-time jobs. The Rude Ranch philosophy was and always would be to help people who wanted to help animals. We just didn't know how many of them there were.

It was a big decision for Bob to leave his secure government job to help animals for nothing but the satisfaction. We were pretty sure the satisfaction wouldn't pay many bills. All the normal questions went through our minds. Did we have enough money? Could we live on one salary and still help animals? Would we be any good at fundraising? Had we completely lost our minds? The last question was one often asked of us over the years; we even asked it of ourselves occasionally.

One thing that helped Bob and me financially was our aforementioned frugal nature. When other people received raises or bonuses they would take a trip, buy a new car or spend the money on something they always wanted. Bob and I would invest the money or pay off some bills. We knew there was something else we wanted to do with our lives and it would probably require significant savings to accomplish this goal. We were a little (make that a lot) nervous, but decided you only lived once and took the plunge.

Now that Bob was soon to be "retired" (or just tired), and we had officially taken the plunge and started our own non-profit organization, it was time to get the word out that we existed. The first task was to start our own newsletter and develop a mailing list of people that supported what we did. Being novices at this endeavor we recruited Denise, a volunteer who transported animals from Delaware to Rude Ranch, to help out with the newsletter. She was a graphics artist and helped develop newsletters for a living.

We laid out the initial format, I wrote the stories and Denise put it all together so it looked good. We created a mailing list that included people who had adopted from us over the years and sent out our first newsletter to about 800 people.

We also did some research on how to handle the inflow of animals into a shelter or sanctuary. We found out we were already following a fairly strict protocol for bringing animals into our house. They would go into a cage for the first two weeks until we could determine if they were healthy and we could complete all their vet work. Then they would go into rooms based on their situation and personality. We started as a cageless sanctuary and it was working great. The cats could run and play in the rooms together and live a somewhat normal life. Introducing new cats to the current residents became sort of an art form. Every cat was different and we had to modify our approach accordingly. Bob only had one cat he failed to integrate with the other cats. That cat was a beautiful white cat named Sam. He loved the dogs, so he became part of their pack. Problem solved!

With the in-take of animals under control, we now had to get organized with regards to paperwork and adoptions. We couldn't keep taking animals in unless we could find new homes for them. We had to develop our own outlet for adoptions. We applied for and were accepted into the PetSmart adoption family. Now we could set up at local PetSmart stores and let people see our kids. As an added bonus, for every adoption we completed at a PetSmart store, they would kick in a donation to Rude Ranch. We also set up "open" hours at the sanctuary for people who wanted to meet the cats in their "natural" environment.

We also realized that when you quit your job and converted your home into an animal sanctuary you had to do some rearranging. We started with the rooms in the basement. One of the rooms was now the quarantine room. The temple room (remember, we bought the house from the Hari Krishnas) was now the general population (adoption) room. The remaining basement room was now our in-take room.

This rearranging also meant something else: everything Bob and I had stored in the basement had to be moved to the third level of the house. By now Bob and I got more exercise schlepping the treadmill around the house than we did from actually using it.

Once we figured out what the rooms would be used for, we started construction. As a no-kill sanctuary, we knew some of the animals would be with us for a long time. They would need more stuff to keep them busy than a couple of litter boxes and a bed.

We hooked up with Joe, our favorite handyman/carpenter. He let his imagination run wild, building climbing poles, ramps and shelves for the cats. He and Bob even built special benches around an aquarium for the cats to watch the fish.

Now we just needed to paint everything. That was when I made a small error in judgment: I let Bob pick the colors. He picked bright yellow for the walls. I didn't have a problem with yellow, until I saw this particular yellow: Actually I squinted, more like needed sunglasses, to look at it on a cloudy day. The cats and dogs stopped cold coming into the rooms because they were blinded by the glaring bright yellow (okay, maybe I was exaggerating a little at this point). I guess I learned my lesson, don't let Bob pick out paint unsupervised.

The Kids Taking a Nap in the General Population Room

Now on to the animals: By this time we had nine personal cats (Tia, Billie Jo, Ashley, Ghost, Maggie, Momma Mia, Cali, Goldie and Bones) and two dogs (Boomer and Bruno) who we dubbed official Rude Ranch permanent residents. We also had several foster cats that were keeping us busy.

Things were starting to get quiet again, which could only mean one thing: I bet you are thinking more cats; no, this time the house was invaded by mice. Yes that's right, a house with more than twenty cats and we had mice running around. We just hoped the cats were catching them and quietly disposing of them. We didn't get that lucky.

It took some effort, but we finally resolved the great mouse invasion when Bob discovered a slight hole where the exhaust for our oven came into the house. Bob plugged the hole, and to our cats' disappointment, the mice were no more. We were never sure why the mice would invade a cat sanctuary anyway; some of us joked that it must be a mouse gang initiation ritual. At least the fun of finding signs of mice all over the house was over.

Illustration Courtesy of Amber Phillips

Then a new project came to us via Baltimore City. There were a lot of cats living in a city park and they were breeding out of control. We began working with a lady who was willing to take care of the colony and help get them fixed. That's where the new agreement Bob and I had with Dr. Harrison came into play.

The first group of cats they wanted us to help were six male cats that had recently joined the colony. They needed to be fixed, so I set up the appointment for a Monday. The cats were dropped off Sunday night, placed in what had been our exercise room (now our quarantine room), loaded up Monday morning and were off to the vet. The whole operation (no pun intended) went pretty well. So well that we set up another appointment, this time for three more males and five females. That's when we started getting busy.

Two days after our "patients" were picked up, we were asked if we could take three more cats that were rescued on behalf of Baltimore City. They were half feral, so they would need to be caged and quarantined. We had a quarantine room; we just didn't have any cages for it yet. That meant we had to take the cages from the office (which had now been dubbed our feral room) and reassemble them downstairs. Notice that we had to carry a lot of stuff up and down the stairs.

We eventually took custody of a torti kitten (Willow), a black and white long-hair (Cordelia) and a huge Russian blue look-alike (Giles). We set them up in the new quarantine room. They were all a little unsure of what was happening to them, but seemed okay with the food service and accommodations. Cordelia, however, seemed especially unhappy. She really made her point clear when she bit me right in the knuckle which promptly swelled up to about three times its normal size. It was off to the doctor for antibiotics and a different approach to handling Cordelia.

A few days later, we had eight more furry guests coming for a three day visit. Seven of these cats would be going to the vet for their spay/neuter surgeries on the following Monday and then going home on Wednesday. They would be staying together in our quarantine room. We moved Giles, Willow and Cordelia into the general population room to make space for our new guests.

The eighth guest was a big tomcat named Mr. Macho. He was caught poaching chickens from a farmer on the Eastern Shore of

Maryland. The farmer wasn't all that happy with this activity and was threatening to put Mr. Macho out of the chicken poaching business permanently. Luckily, a cat friendly person took pity on the little poacher and made arrangements to bring him to Rude Ranch. We set Mr. Macho up with a cage in the feral room. Shortly after his arrival, we found out why he had such a tough sounding name. We couldn't go near his cage without fear of him reaching out and clawing at us.

Soon it was time for our "visiting" cats to make the trip to the vet for their life changing alterations. Bob loaded them up for the trip and got them all checked in at the clinic. On his way out the door Lauree, one of the vet techs, mentioned there was a feral cat loose in the basement of the building. Could he help? Bob headed to the basement with Lauree to evaluate the situation. They found the cat hiding in a room and thought their best option was to close the door to confine her in that area.

Bob made several attempts to catch the cat, but she just wasn't falling for his charm. Bob was running a little late for work; so, he told Lauree he would come back later that day better prepared to catch the cat. Then they went to leave the room. Oops, no door knob on their side of the door. Lauree had a brief moment of panic: "I'm locked in a room with this crazy cat guy!!!" Bob hoped the vet staff would eventually miss Lauree and come looking for her. They finally escaped from the room by jiggling the door enough to work it open. Crisis averted.

When Bob returned to pick up our visitors, the escaped feral cat had already been captured. All Bob had to do was bring our visitors home for recovery. It was nice to have a quiet day once in awhile.

That night we got a call from the people doing the trapping in Baltimore City. They had two more kittens, both girls, could we take them?

Well, we were out of cages again, but if we let Mr. Macho loose in the feral room, we could use his crate for one cat and then use Bruno's old crate for the other one. Okay, so Buffy and Faith were on their way. We had started working on a *Buffy the Vampire Slayer* naming convention and still had a few names to use up.

Due to the shortage of cages, we decided to try putting the kittens in the cage with Willow. They were from the same colony and most likely knew each other. Bob pulled the first kitten out. I checked; nope this was a boy, oh well, we'd put him into the crate in the in-take room. Okay, we got the second kitten out, thinking this one had to be a female. I "lifted the tail." Ummm, this one was a boy too. Okay, maybe I screwed up on the other kitten. We went back and checked. Nope, it was still a boy. Now Bob and I were no experts at some of this stuff, but we were pretty sure we could tell the difference between a boy and a girl, so instead of a Buffy and Faith, we now had Angel and Xander. Willow wasn't thrilled with either one of them. So they both went into cages in the in-take room.

The following day started without incident. I did my morning rounds and everyone was accounted for in their respective rooms; good, no problems. At lunch Bob brought a couple of coworkers over to play with the cats. He decided to introduce them to the guest cats and then noticed that where there should have been seven cats in the room, there were only five. Okay, modern math or not, we were short two cats. Then he noticed the window in the room was open about a foot from the top. Bob called me at work: "Please tell me that two of the visiting cats got loose in the house today!" That wasn't a good sign. Somehow the cats managed to open an unlatched window and escaped from the quarantine room. (In a house where Bob and I had trouble getting most of the windows opened, these cats managed to find the one window that operated smoothly.) I rushed home from work, while Bob abandoned his coworkers to start a patterned search of our neighborhood.

We spent the next seven hours going through our neighbors' yards, barns and outbuildings looking for these two cats. Did you know it was possible to get poison ivy in the winter? You also tend to get a lot of strange looks from people when you emerge from their barn with a can of cat food and a kitty carrier in your hand. Despite our best efforts, we had no luck finding the cats.

We did meet a lot of neighbors we hadn't met before. Everyone was very cooperative and wished us luck in our search. They all promised to call if they saw any cats roaming about. We were afraid to guess what they thought about their new neighbors that wandered through their barns looking for cats.

We finally had to give up the search and try a different strategy. We put food on the front step, set our traps at strategic locations on the property and hoped for the best. Around 7:30 that night, we thought we got lucky. One of the cats was eating on the front step. Yippeee!!! He was okay, and he was back. All we had to do was walk out the front door and scoop him up. Unfortunately, it didn't work that way; as soon as we touched the front door, the cat took off. Then we thought we would get lucky out back. The other escapee was almost in the trap we had placed near the window. Then Ghost rushed up to the window and the cat ran into the woods.

Now the moment of truth had arrived: the cats' parents showed up expecting to pick up seven cats. We had to tell them they could only pick up five of them, but we knew the other two were in the vicinity. And yes, we were stupid enough to assume cats couldn't open a window.

While we were explaining this to the parents, one of the cats happened to trot by. He wasn't keen on coming to the other people either, but we did eventually catch him. Then we saw the second cat. He was taking off for our next door neighbor's stable. We hoped the neighbors didn't mind too much that Bob kind of broke their fence as he was climbing over it. We also hoped they didn't mind all the flashlights shining in their yard (it was close to midnight by now). After all, it was perfectly normal to run around your neighbor's yard yelling "here kitty kitty" at midnight.

We eventually concluded there was no way we were going to catch this cat that night. However, he had a weakness for food. So we set the trap again, and went to bed hoping he would be waiting for us in the morning (okay, later in the morning).

Morning arrived and I cautiously went out the front door to check the trap. There was a cat in it! Yes!!! Except it was someone else's cat, "%$#&&"! We would have to try again later.

Evening arrived and we set the trap again. While putting the rest of the kids to bed I was attracted to the front of the house when I noticed several of the Rude Cats staring at the front door (or it could have been the howling coming from the front step that attracted my attention).

At first I couldn't tell whether the cat was mad because he was in the trap or because half of his dinner was still on the front step. Either way, as soon as Bob and I opened the trap, the cat that had hissed and run from us outside, walked out of the trap, rubbed up against us and rolled over for tummy rubs. Why couldn't he have done that yesterday!

Buffy the Feather Slayer

It was a huge milestone for Rude Ranch! We received our approval as a permanent IRS approved non-profit charity! Up to this point we had a temporary status as a charity until all our paperwork was reviewed and approved. Now we could really start moving forward with recruiting volunteers, working on the fundraising and trying to find more creative ways to find homes for the kids we took into Rude Ranch. After all, we were running out of friends and family to adopt our rescued cats.

We thought there would have been some sort of fanfare or at least a little party to mark the occasion. But, it was just a quick high five between Bob and me and then back to taking care of the animals.

It was around that time when Bob worked his last day at the Census Bureau after nearly seventeen years. It was sort of a surreal moment. Were we really doing this? Well, it was too late to turn back now. Bob's coworkers sent him on his way with a party at the officer's club at Andrews Air Force Base. They even got together and bought him an appropriate farewell gift. Rather than the typical clock, watch or plaque, Bob received his very own microscope. I will confess that his coworkers consulted with me on the gift. I thought it might come in handy in his new line of work.

Now that Bob could focus on the animals full-time, we suddenly started getting more requests. One such request was for a little twelve week old kitten that was rescued from Hanover Street in Baltimore City. Her fur was long and snowy white, and she was in desperate need of a bath. It was no easy task to bathe a kitten, especially a kitten that had just been rescued from a feral colony. We finally managed to get most of the crud off her without losing too much of our own blood. To show her appreciation, she rolled around in her litter box as soon as we put her back in her cage (and of course, it was clumping litter). That earned her four more baths. This time we remembered to take up the litter before putting her back in the cage (unlike old dogs, we could learn from our mistakes). At least she smelled really good now. This little ball of fluff was dubbed "Buffy the Feather Slayer" (Buffy) to continue our *Buffy the Vampire Slayer* series of cats.

A few days later we got another call: Buffy's sister Faith had been trapped and was on her way to the vet. Could we take her? We had the rest of the crew, so why not. Our main problem was a shortage of cages. We always had more cats coming into Rude Ranch than we had cages to quarantine them. We were getting tired of using our bathrooms as overflow quarantine rooms. We either had to buy more cages or stop taking in so many new cats. We decided it was time to write our first grant proposal; after all, we now had our charity status and might qualify for funding on projects like this.

We applied to PetSmart Charities for a grant to purchase twenty-four cat condos that would become our in-take cages for new cats and kittens. The whole process was a little overwhelming with a lot of paperwork and a lot of waiting. It was all worth it though; we were approved for the grant and had our new cages installed a few weeks later.

By now Buffy was making incredible progress towards wanting attention from Bob and me. It was time to find her a home. After some careful thought about how to accomplish this, Bob put a pretty red ribbon on Buffy and she became my early Christmas present. You would think he could be more creative; after all, we already had a lot of cats. I think Bob just forgot to get me something for Christmas and this was his quick, panicked attempt to avoid getting whacked by the infamous rolling pin. It worked.

Buffy the Christmas Present

A few days later, we received another call: a sibling to Buffy and Faith had been caught. Could we take it? Charity moved in the next day.

Then we received a call around midnight from a volunteer at Save A Life. Four kittens had been dumped at her house and she couldn't take care of them. Could Bob and I help? It was amazing what you would agree to, in the middle of the night, when you were half asleep. Spike, Sweetie, LB, and Fluff moved into our in-take room.

Two days later, we received another call. Someone had dropped off two, four week old kittens in front of the Annapolis PetSmart. Could we take them? Soon Duchess and Muffy were residing in our living room. Now when someone asked me how many cats we had, I started counting on my fingers and toes.

I knew Bob had quit his job to work full-time with the animals, but this was getting ridiculous. Did someone put out a flyer that we were looking for animals? I guess we should have taken things a little slower at first.

Luckily we had a cat show on the horizon. We had six kittens and one cat that were ready to be adopted. We were really hoping some of them would find a home at the show and make room for the many other cats and kittens waiting for space at Rude Ranch. The only concern about the show was this particular weekend happened to be Easter. We were a little nervous about the turnout and whether we would place many animals. The show was also overbooked and was short on space. We could fit all our stuff in the area allocated to us, but it would be a tight squeeze. Fortunately, we found homes for Spike, Sweetie, LB and Fluff. Also, there were several inquiries about Faith and Charity, but nothing that looked very promising.

By the summer of 2001 things were moving at a rapid pace. We really should slow down and do a little more planning before we took in more animals. After all, I had run out of fingers and toes and was forced to resort to using Bob's fingers to keep track of all the animals. I had to devise a better plan before expanding to Bob's toes. Let's just say it's not a place I really wanted to go and leave it at that.

Sophie and Her Kids

Things were really starting to get busy now. We were hoping for a break in the phone calls, but we didn't have that kind of luck. Instead we got a call from a lady referred to us by our vet. A stray cat had moved in under her deck. She felt sorry for the little cat and had been feeding her for awhile. Now she was getting big, as in had a hot date and was in a family way big. Could we take her?

We took one look at Miss Sophie when she arrived and we agreed. She was in a family way, big time. So we set up a cage with towels and a "birthing box" in our quarantine room. She promptly buried all the towels in her litter box. We weren't sure if it was a comment on our choice of fabric softener or just an odd habit. Judging from her size, we felt the "blessed event" couldn't be far off.

We did some basic vet work and found that not only was she really pregnant, she also tested positive for the feline immunodeficiency virus (FIV). This was our first experience with a cat testing positive for FIV. We did some research and found that FIV was not as bad as feline leukemia, but she would still have to be kept separate from other cats that didn't have the disease. It could be transmitted to other cats through a bite wound. There was also a good possibility her kittens would contract the disease.

We weren't sure what to do at first, but we did know putting her to sleep wasn't an option. We started out to be a no-kill sanctuary and had no plans to change our philosophy. We settled in to wait for the "blessed event." It really shouldn't be long now; she was bigger than a basketball. Instead of giving birth, she just kept getting bigger. We were starting to wonder just what Sophie would give birth to. We assumed kittens, but judging from her size, it could be almost anything.

Then one morning, it happened. By 6 a.m., Sophie had given birth to two kittens. Bob went out to run some errands and when he returned there were three kittens. The fourth kitten was born at three in the afternoon. These kittens were HUGE. At twelve hours old, they were already the size of the average two week old kittens! I guess that's why Sophie was so big; she just didn't want to give birth and start raising a family as a single mom.

These kittens were not only big, but they were also the healthiest kittens we had seen in a long time. They were all solid black like their mother. Sophie was a very nurturing and protective mother. She would let Bob and me handle the kittens, but any animal that dared to come near them took their life into their paws.

Boomer found that out the hard way one day when he snuck into her room to steal some food. Boomer was nowhere near the kittens, but Sophie wasn't taking any chances. She launched an airborne offensive attack, jumping onto Boomer from the window sill with all claws extended. Boomer made the decision that Sophie's food didn't look all that appetizing anymore. He turned tail and ran out the door with Sophie swatting at his butt the whole way. We eventually found Boomer huddled under our bed. He didn't try sneaking into that room again for a long time.

Sophie's kittens were soon big enough we could tell them apart. We named them Stevie, Bear, Chester and Boots. They grew quickly and were having a blast running around the room.

As they grew, we knew it was time to regroup and figure out what to do with FIV positive cats. We hadn't really planned for this one and couldn't keep them in the quarantine room forever. Although we originally planned to keep the sanctuary in the basement of our house, we decided we really didn't need four bedrooms just for Bob and me. After all, we could only sleep in one room at a time. We would move Sophie and her kids upstairs to what had been our exercise room. We really weren't using the treadmill all that much anyway. It did make a good clothes rack though.

With that decided, it was time to give Joe the handyman a call. Bob and Joe started working to convert two of the bedrooms upstairs into cat rooms. The FIV cats would be in the exercise room and the feral cats would be moved to my sewing room. Bob was getting tired of sharing his office, our current feral room, with ten cats that hated humans anyway.

The FIV room was the priority and was finished first. Sophie and her kids were easy to move and quickly settled into their new digs with fancy ramps to play on and nice cubby holes to sleep in.

Loki in One of the Upstairs Cat Rooms

In the meantime, we finally had a breakthrough with Mr. Macho. The cat that instilled fear in the hearts of all decided we weren't so bad. It started when he escaped from his cage in the office. We thought it was probably time to let him out anyway and we really didn't relish the idea of re-capturing him. He eventually picked the top of the PC monitor as his domain. From that vantage point he could keep an eye on everything in the room and intimidate whoever was using the PC. Whenever anyone sat at the computer he would hang over the top of the monitor with a menacing look on his face. It made it a little difficult to focus on our work wondering if he'd suddenly launch an attack.

One night Bob was sitting at the PC doing some important sanctuary work (I think it was either solitaire or mahjong) and snacking on some cheddar cheese, all the time wondering if Mr. Macho was going to attach himself to his face. Then Mr. Macho reached down and snagged himself a piece of cheese right out of Bob's hand. Bob thought what the heck and carefully extended a piece of cheese to him. Pretty soon Mr. Macho was eating cheese out of Bob's hand and rolling over for tummy rubs. That was a new method of socializing cats we hadn't tried before. I guess it was "the power of cheese." (Bob should be ashamed of himself for not figuring that one out. Remember, he was from Wisconsin, the cheese state.)

Xander and Friends

Xander's story with us started in March, 2000. He was one of the cats rescued near Baltimore, Maryland. He was named as part of our famed *Buffy the Vampire Slayer* series of cats (we also had a Buffy, Willow, Cordelia, Giles, Angel, and Faith. Then we ran out of time to watch the show and ran out of characters).

Xander came in as a four month old feral kitten and promptly tore Bob and me to pieces every chance he got. Eventually we worked out an agreement; we would leave him alone and he wouldn't try to shred us.

Then it was time for Xander and his brother Angel to get fixed. At this point they were the equivalent of human fifteen year old boys with raging hormones. They were obnoxious, messy and a general pain in the neck. We made an appointment with the vet to take care of these problems.

The night before their surgeries, we dutifully took their food and water up and made sure we would be able to catch them in the morning. Unfortunately, both cats were on to us. When we went to "stuff" the boys into carriers in the morning, Angel cooperated until I had him just inches away from the carrier. Then he twisted around, bit me, dug in with all four paws and took off to hide behind Mr. Macho. Xander also put on a good show. He started running around the room at full speed. Then he started hissing and growling. Maybe today was not the day to take them in for their surgeries. We would regroup and come up with a better plan.

We made an appointment for the following week. We picked up knock out pills from the vet. The plan was to mix the pills in their food. The pills would take affect in about an hour and the cats would be groggy for at least a couple of hours after that; long enough to get them into special cages and cart them off to the vet before they knew what was happening. We got lucky with Angel. He wolfed his food down like there was no tomorrow. Unfortunately, Xander suspected something and refused to eat. Taz, however, did eat his food and took a nice long nap afterwards.

Now we were down to a battle of wills, Bob and me against Xander. It was time to pull out the heavy artillery. We mixed up another concoction using chicken baby food. Most cats couldn't resist baby food. Xander could.

This called for another plan of action, and it wouldn't be pretty. We armed ourselves with the standard full body armor. We removed all breakables from the vicinity. We got our heavy towels ready. Oops, he shredded the towels. We would go with heavy sweatshirts instead. After a fair amount of growling and hissing on Xander's part, we had him rolled up in a sweatshirt and inside a wire cage. By now Angel was comfortably sleeping and an easy mark to stuff into the other cage.

Fortunately, Angel, Xander and the vet all survived their respective ordeals. By the time they arrived back home, the kittens were sleepy and only a little ticked off at us. They did get even with us the next day, however, when they ripped open an extra bag of kitty litter, spread it all over the floor and encouraged the rest of the cats to use the pile 'o litter instead of the litter box.

During all of this fun, Bob and Joe were busy putting the finishing touches on the new feral room. The dreaded day had arrived; it was time to move the feral cats from our office to their new room. It was also time for me to say good-bye to my sewing room forever; it was now the official feral room. As always, when moving ten cats that don't want to be moved, madness ensued. We learned it was possible for a cat not only to climb drywall, but also to balance on the top of a door frame. We set new records for the number of curse words uttered in a single breathe. However, Bob and I prevailed and these guys were eventually moved to their new room upstairs.

That led to a new adventure: Every now and then you hear a story about how a cat or dog traveled back to its original home after the family moved miles away. Well, with Xander it was a matter of traveling back downstairs to "his" room. After a few weeks in the new feral room, we noticed that whenever someone opened the door, Xander would be right there, ready to shoot out on them.

Usually he wouldn't make it too far and we could herd him back into the feral room. Then he caught a lucky break. The door knob broke. The part that went into the door frame and held the door shut was jammed. People coming and going from the room didn't know this, but somehow Xander figured it out and seized the opportunity. The door would drift open a little and his paw would go into the small crack and open it the rest of the way. Most of the time the cats in the room would be too frightened to explore very far, and as soon as they heard someone coming, would run back into the room. But not Xander! He would take off for his old room downstairs. If he didn't think he could make it into that room, he would head for cover under the couch in the family room.

Every time we put Xander back in the feral room, he became more determined to get out. One time he got out of the room and tried to make it downstairs to his old room (at least we think that was his game plan). Instead, I headed him off at the stairway and he ran into the master bedroom. That was completely new territory for Xander. He didn't quite know what to do and stopped cold in the middle of the room.

We think he was planning to turn around and run back to the feral room, but now he had another problem, Billie Jo, the enforcer. Billie Jo wasn't going to let him by without some discomfort on Xander's part, so he ran further into the room. The only problem with that plan was Ashley, the bully, was waiting for him. At that point Xander decided running under the bed was his best bet for survival.

Thus began what became known as the "Summer of Catching Xander." We saw him every day. He became best friends with Buffy. He eventually worked out an agreement with Ashley and Billie Jo. Tia (The Queen) gave him the once over and deemed him beneath her, but grudgingly left him alone. We just couldn't catch him to put him back in his room. He eventually settled into our closet and seemed content hanging out there.

The time finally came when we had to do something with Xander. With him running loose in the house we couldn't make any progress towards socializing him. It was either do something soon or resign ourselves to living with a cat we couldn't touch. We decided to set up a dog crate in our bedroom and let Xander live there until we could convince him to tolerate us humans.

One night we decided it was now or never, and set out to capture Xander. Our goal was to catch him and put him in the dog crate. We started out with luck on our side; he was sitting in the middle of our bedroom. We shut the bedroom door and began the "Great Xander Capture."

First we flushed him out from under the bed. Then we flushed him (not literally) from behind the toilet. Then we thought we had him. He went into the closet. At that point Bob was in the lead. He managed to get a grip on him, but Xander would have none of it and was putting up a fight. Bob wasn't going to get him bare-handed; so, being a level headed kind of guy, he improvised. He grabbed my bath robe and wrapped it around Xander and triumphantly carried him out of the closet. There was only one problem: one very critical part of Xander's anatomy was exposed and that part was shooting a pretty steady stream of urine across my clothes (you know, the good work clothes) as Bob was bringing him out of the closet.

At least Xander was now resting comfortably in his crate, but Bob and I had four loads of laundry ahead of us. Some of the other cats were wondering why Xander was now hanging out in a dog crate. Bones decided to make one of his patented moves and started stealing food out of Xander's cage. Billie Jo, who was never really a fan of Xander's in the first place, sat on top of the crate and appeared to be ridiculing him. At least he seemed to be settled into his little bed and trying to make the best of the situation.

Now we were ready to start working with Xander. The first day went about as well as we could expect. He hissed a little and wasn't really thrilled with our plans for him. The second day he escaped from the crate when I fed him his dinner. He went right back into the closet.

As Bob followed in an attempt to recapture the little guy, I told him that if he and Xander did the same thing as last time, I was going to run Bob through the washer four times. At least I got my robe back urine-free that time.

The rest of the summer progressed in a similar manner. Xander would escape and we would capture him and put him back in the crate. We never had a cat so adept at escaping before. No matter what we did, he would either sneak by us when we were cleaning his cage, or figure out a way to escape on his own. We were a little suspicious that Buffy may have been lending him a hand, but we never had any proof. Then he discovered the laser pointer. He became so obsessed with this new toy he didn't care who was watching. He would happily play with the moving red dot no matter what was happening around him. Soon he would let me scratch his ears while he was waiting for his beloved red dot to reappear. From there we moved on to tummy rubs.

Eventually, Xander was out of the crate full-time and playfully helped me get ready for work every morning. He still loved his laser pointer, but was always a little leery of Billie Jo. He would always cringe a little whenever Bob petted him. I guess he never forgave him for the whole laundry incident.

Tommy & Ceasar Arrive

Things were still moving along on the rescue front while we were getting Xander under control. We even had some new residents at Rude Ranch.

One was Greyson who came to us via a Great Dane Rescue. They found him when they rescued a Great Dane that had been abandoned in a house. Greyson was hanging out with the Great Dane and they just couldn't leave the cat behind. They weren't set up to handle cats, so they made a call to Rude Ranch. Did we have room for a big, loveable cat? That was how Greyson came to live with us.

One of the other new arrivals came to us by way of Prince George's Feral Friends. This guy's name was Tommy. When we saw him we had to admit he had it all: looks, personality, attitude, and a history that could have come from a tabloid. Tommy was originally picked up at Andrews Air Force Base (you know, the place where the president parked his plane). The lady who brought Tommy to Rude Ranch caught us by surprise when she told us his story. Tommy's previous mom was a prostitute. After his home was raided by the police, he ended up wandering the Air Force base. We can only imagine the stories Tommy could tell us if only he could talk; he may end up writing a book of his own one day.

Tommy was a real nut right from the start. He loved chasing and attacking the vacuum cleaner, especially when it was running. He thought riding Bruno around the house would be a great idea (Bruno didn't agree). He even stole a graham cracker from a nine month old baby. Considering all of his antics, it only made sense to use him for a TV spot to advertise the sanctuary.

"Bad Boy" Tommy

We got lucky and landed a five minute spot on a news show highlighting animals available for adoption. Tommy and another kitten were chosen as the most photogenic cats for the spot. When the time came for them to strut their stuff, the kitten was in the middle of coughing up a hairball and couldn't go on air. Tommy seized the opportunity, and when the camera lights went on, Tommy turned on the charm. When the interviewer said he was allergic to cats, Tommy wanted to make sure by jumping onto his lap and rubbing all over him. The interviewer wasn't kidding; we think he survived the sneezing fit, but we weren't so sure about his swollen eyes. Maybe they would recruit someone else to handle the cats next time.

That summer the dog population at Rude Ranch increased by one. It all started innocently enough: Bill, the owner of the Save A Life shelter, saw a dog running around a shopping center parking lot. He picked up the dog and brought it back to the shelter. The dog's collar had his name, Ceasar, and his parents' phone number. Bill contacted them and happily returned Ceasar to his home. Ceasar promptly ran away again and almost beat Bill back to the shelter. Obviously these people were having a tough time containing Ceasar the escape artist.

Ceasar the Border Collie

After a few more trips like that, Bill thought Ceasar needed a home that could do a little better job of containing this little run-away. He also knew Bob and I were thinking about adopting another dog as a pal for Bruno. Boomer just couldn't keep up with the type of play Bruno craved. Ceasar was a Border Collie/Siberian Husky mix and would have no problem keeping up with Bruno. He was also very cat friendly, so that sealed the deal and Ceasar came to live with us.

Ceasar had a lot of good habits when we brought him home. He didn't jump on the furniture, he didn't pee in the house, he would go into a crate without making a fuss, and he didn't jump up on the table to get food. These were all good qualities in a dog. We were hoping these qualities would rub off on Boomer and Bruno rather than their bad habits rubbing off on Ceasar.

Ceasar's first meeting with Bruno went okay; there was the typical sniffing and tree marking. Bruno realized he could actually play with this dog without hurting him, and the race was on. It took two head-on, full-speed, Bruno tackles before Ceasar figured out he needed to run really fast and make a lot of turns. It looked like this relationship was going to work out great.

Ceasar also loved the cats, a good quality for a dog to have when living at a cat sanctuary. He seemed to think that the kitten grooming was his specialty. Whenever we saw a sopping wet kitten slinking across the floor, we knew Ceasar had been at work.

Never let it be said we didn't take the animals' feelings into consideration at Rude Ranch. If Ceasar wanted kittens to groom, we would do our best to accommodate him. We took custody of a litter of barn kittens shortly after Ceasar settled into our home. They didn't care for us humans much at first, but they loved Ceasar. Mr. Fizzy, Mr. Fuzzy, Oingo, Boingo, Bongo and Hope were nothing more than little balls of fluff. Ceasar could barely keep up with his new grooming duties. He'd lay on the floor with the kittens and they'd crawl all over him like a jungle gym.

Soon Ceasar's new charges were ready to find forever homes. He reluctantly gave them permission to go to the Friskies cat show that weekend. All but one of his little kittens found new homes at the show. The only reason the sixth kitten wasn't adopted along with his siblings was because Lauree, one of the vet techs at the clinic, had fallen in love with him. She met him when he was getting his neuter surgery. When Bob picked the kittens up after their surgery, Lauree started asking questions about Mr. Fuzzy. Bob had a feeling where the conversation was going, and he was right, Lauree wanted Mr. Fuzzy (now known as Elliot).

We had another surprise at the Friskies cat show. The Friskies people were interested in Tommy. They thought he was a complete and total nut and had serious potential for commercial work. They talked to us extensively about adding him to their traveling show and doing commercials for them. It was looking like it would happen, but in the end, they just didn't have space to add another cat to their program. A close brush with fame, but it wasn't meant to be. Tommy wasn't fazed at all by his missed opportunity. He was just happy Friskies donated all the extra food from the cat show to Rude Ranch.

For some reason, the cat shows were close together that year. A couple of weeks later, another show was being held at the Timonium State Fairgrounds. By a stroke of luck, we also landed a TV spot to promote the shelter the same day. That worked out well for everyone; both the shelter and the cat show got extra advertising. Bob and I just had to pull it off. You see there was one major glitch; the TV station was in Washington D.C. and the cat show was north of Baltimore. Everything was happening between seven and eight in the morning. The logistics just weren't working out.

It was time to divide and conquer. I took Tommy (our budding star) and Tiger, one of our kittens, to the TV station. Bob loaded up all our other cats and headed for the Save A Life shelter to help load their cats. When I finished at the TV station, I would race to the fairgrounds to set up. If there was a problem, Bob would page me, and I would head to the shelter instead. Sounded reasonable, right?

For my part, I set out for the TV station, and didn't get lost. That was a good start. However, true to form, Tommy yakked three blocks from the station. I cleaned up Tommy and got both cats into the TV station. When it was time to go on air, Tommy was sitting in my lap, with Tiger in a carrier at my feet.

While the interviewer and I were talking, the producer decided to crawl under the line of the camera to get Tiger out of her carrier and put her in the interviewer's lap. I was trying to carry on an intelligent conversation (which for me was a miracle anyway) while watching the show going on under the camera. In the end, a very surprised Tiger found herself digging into the interviewer's lap and was hanging on for dear life. Oh yeah, this was the guy we had before who was allergic to cats.

With the interview over, I was now supposed to race up to the cat show. I hadn't heard from Bob so I figured everything was going well. I got within ten miles of the cat show when my pager went off. If I remembered the plan right, my pager going off meant Bob was having trouble at the shelter and I was to go there to help. I turned around on the freeway and headed back to the shelter, all the while trying to get a hold of Bob. I couldn't get an answer on his phone, so I paged him. We played "freeway pager tag" for quite a while. When we finally managed to hook up, I found out the reason Bob paged me; they got a late start from the shelter, but were on their way. Now I was headed the wrong direction and had to turn around, again! Fortunately, Tommy managed not to puke during any of this.

Most of our foster kids did well and found homes at the cat show. Ceasar was a little disappointed, but we assured him he would have more kittens to take care of soon. Tommy was a big hit at the cat show too. He even started a job as a cat tree model for "Polkat Productions," one of the vendors at the show. Tommy perched at the top of one of the trees and started drawing people over to buy them. Maybe we could work out a deal for discounted cat trees?

Quiver and Friends

We were adding a lot of cats to Rude Ranch without a whole lot of thought to handling the yearly exams for our kids. As caring, responsible pet parents we realized all the animals would need annual examinations to monitor their overall health. Being cheap (frugal), we wanted to take advantage of the multiple pet discount our vet offered, meaning all the animals would go in together. Yes, we were stupid enough to bring three dogs and ten cats to the vet at the same time. The following events led us to the realization we needed to change our approach to vet care.

After the usual bloodshed involved with getting everyone loaded up, we proceeded to the vet clinic. Upon our arrival, Boomer promptly peed on the front door. I ushered him out to the curb, where he managed to provide another urine sample for the vet. Way to go Boomer!

To keep the waiting room from overcrowding, we were immediately ushered into two exam rooms, the cats in one, and the dogs in the other. Ceasar was a little nervous, actually more than a little nervous, like mess all over the floor nervous. The vet tech decided it wasn't necessary to get a temperature on Ceasar after that. I guess I couldn't blame her.

Now it was time to draw blood for the dogs' heart worm tests. Boomer and Ceasar did surprisingly well. Then it was Bruno's turn. Did I mention that Bruno didn't like to be restrained for any reason? I was pretty sure donating blood wouldn't be any different. They managed to get blood out of the big guy, but I was a little worried the assisting vet tech would wind up with a concussion. Bruno did a major head butt on his face and it looked like it was more than a little painful. Then Dr. Theresa Roller came in to examine the dogs and Boomer made a run for it through the open door. Four of us chased Boomer all over the building, ending with Bob doing an impressive diving tackle to finally catch him (actually, I think Bob may have just tripped, but I'll give him credit for the grab anyway).

Once we recovered Boomer, Dr. Roller was able to complete the dogs' examinations. They all got a clean bill of health. We thought it would be best to put the dogs in a kennel while Dr. Roller examined the cats. Bob volunteered to escort the dogs and somehow managed to lock himself inside the kennel. Apparently, they only opened from the outside to prevent dogs from escaping (I bet Bob wished he had known that before he locked himself inside). The staff told me they would charge double for kenneling Bob, so I reclaimed him.

The cats were next. For some reason the cats were all amazingly cooperative and well mannered for their exams. Dr. Roller was able to crank through all ten quickly and pronounced them all healthy. A major event concluded with only minor adventures. It did lead us to the realization we had to modify our approach to vet care. With the way we were expanding our animal population, we'd be visiting the vet all the time. At least we had some time to contemplate what to do, now that we had the exams completed for that year.

On the rescue front, we had a population explosion at the end of September. We took in nine kittens from another rescuer who had a family emergency. That took us to a total of twelve kittens and twenty sanctuary cats. That was the easy part. The harder part was what to do with Harpo and Elvis, two new cats that tested positive for feline leukemia, also known as FELV.

Like the FIV positive cats, these two would need to be kept physically separate from the other cats. While many shelters and sanctuaries euthanize FELV cats, we planned to let them have fun and live out their lives until the disease caught up with them. Bob's first two cats had leukemia and they had fun right up until the disease took them.

The only question was where would we keep them? We had two leukemia cats living in a bathroom and we were getting calls from other groups asking us to take more. We would definitely need more space for them if we planned to have a leukemia program. We gave it some thought and realized we still had one room left in the house that we could use for the cats. The bedroom next to ours was being used to keep the litter boxes for our cats. We could move their litter boxes to one of the walk-in closets in our bedroom. The cats would have easy access and I didn't really care either, since I put the litter boxes in Bob's closet. He was already using more than his pre-nuptually agreed upon eighteen inches of closet space anyway.

Now that the room was empty, Bob and Joe were back on the job converting the last extra bedroom we had into the leukemia room. They had the room completed in just under a week. I guess they had the routine down pat by now.

We moved Elvis and Harpo into their new room. They settled in quickly and had a blast playing on the ramps and hanging out with each other. It was a lot of space for two cats, but we knew it would only be a matter of time before they had some new buddies.

Then we ran into a serious problem with one of our new kittens. Babbette started having grand mal seizures. Per "Murphy's Law" she started having the seizures after the regular vet was closed, necessitating a trip to the emergency vet (translation: it was going to cost a lot of money).

Although they couldn't figure out what was causing her seizures, they told us her temperature would go up shortly before she had one. They recommended giving her antibiotics, watching her carefully and giving her a shot of valium when her temperature started going up. Of course, the only way to tell if her temperature was going up was to take it the old fashioned way. We would have to keep sticking a thermometer where the sun doesn't shine. We spent the next week chasing this poor little kitten around with a digital thermometer and a syringe full of valium. We only thought of using it on ourselves five or six times.

Babbette came through it all without any permanent damage. The only real sign she wasn't quite right was that she sometimes forgot to put her tongue back in her mouth. At least that looked endearing on a kitten. We never did identify the cause of her seizures, but she stopped having them; so, we decided to just be happy.

It was around this time another cat came into our feral program. We received a call from a lady who was trying to spay/neuter and feed cats in Patterson Park in Baltimore City. We weren't real familiar with Patterson Park, but we did know that by reputation, this was a pretty rough area of Baltimore City. As soon as she caught the cat she knew he had been abused. He had a nasty looking wound between his shoulder blades and seemed to be in a lot of pain. She wanted to help him, but didn't have a place for him. Could we take him? We said yes and made arrangements to get him to Rude Ranch.

The original plan was for her to meet us at the Save A Life shelter which was midway between our place and Baltimore. Unfortunately the cat, who she had named Quiver, got loose in her house and she couldn't catch him. Could she bring him to our house once she rounded him up? She finally caught the little guy and called to let us know she was on her way. We gave her directions and expected her to arrive around 7 p.m.

We soon found out she had never driven outside of Baltimore City before, let alone into the "horse country" where Bob and I lived. She was so freaked out by the winding roads and lack of street lights that a forty-five minute drive turned into a three and a half-hour ordeal. A somewhat shaken Quiver arrived at our house at 10:30 that night.

The next step was to get Quiver's wound fixed and get him neutered. We would need to transport him in a trap to allow the vet tech to safely sedate him. Getting him into the trap involved a twenty minute chase around the basement, ending with Quiver wrapped up in a blanket, and being dropped upside down into the trap.

We hoped he would do better at the vet's office. We found out Quiver not only didn't do any better, now he owed Dr. Harrison a pair of pants. They thought Quiver was adequately sedated in preparation for his surgery, but Quiver thought otherwise. Before they could administer the rest of his sedatives, he jumped off the surgery table and led Dr. Harrison and staff on a merry chase around the surgery room. They finally captured Quiver when he wrapped himself around

Dr. Harrison's leg. That gave the vet tech a chance to administer heavier sedation and continue with Quiver's surgery. That was a little more excitement than your average neuter surgery. Dr. Harrison did mention that this was the first time, in his twenty years as a vet, he had to run home at lunch to change his pants.

It turned out Quiver's wound was caused by a twenty-two caliber bullet lodged between his shoulder blades. It had abscessed and was pretty badly infected. At least the bullet was out and we could start with the fun of medicating a cat that didn't want us anywhere near him. It went fairly well: Bob would corner him in one of the cubby holes, carefully grab him by the scruff, and then give him his shot in the butt.

We all survived the Quiver excitement and now it was our turn to have fun with Greyson, the cat we took in from the Great Dane rescue. For almost two months we'd been fighting a battle of wills with him and he was winning.

Greyson liked to sleep on top of the furnace. That wouldn't be a huge problem except he turned the furnace off on the way up. We had bi-fold doors to the furnace area, but he would break in by prying them open. When he opened the doors, it also gave the rest of the cats access to the area between the floors of the house. Although I wasn't an expert on house construction, I didn't think the space between the floors of the house was the best place for cats to hang out. Additionally, once they got between the floors we never knew where the cats would end up: After one of Greyson's break-ins, Tommy ended up trapped under the crawl space in the kitchen, Faith came out from the little door that hid the outside water shut-off valve, and Charity spent three days somewhere between the floors of the house.

We made several attempts to thwart Greyson. We started with a bungee cord wrapped around the door. That didn't slow him down at all. We put a fifty pound bag of kitty litter in front of the door. He gutted the bag and pushed it out of the way. The other cats used it as a litter box. We put a trash can holding 200 pounds of kitty litter in front of the door. He pushed in between the trash can and the door and managed to open it enough to squeeze inside. Now we were getting serious. We were either going to stop him or enter him into the kitty power lifting competitions.

Our next attempt was to put a slide latch on the door. He put his paw under the door and jiggled it until the latch moved enough so he could open the door. We put more slide latches on the door. He just laughed at us. Then we mounted our final assault; we got slide latches that were used on gates and drilled holes down into the concrete floor. It took two drill bits and a lot of grunting from Bob, but we finally had what we thought was a Greyson-proof security system. That had him stumped, but every day he sat and stared at the doors. We knew he was working on a plan to get past the bolts. We also knew he would get even with us for installing them in the first place. That was what really had us worried.

Volunteers Invade
Rude Ranch

As we moved through 2002, Bob and I were starting to get the hang of running Rude Ranch. We forged agreements with various animal shelters and animal control agencies to take animals they would normally have to euthanize. We were also recruiting volunteers to help with the massive amount of work involved with running an animal sanctuary, and we were even getting a little better at raising money.

As Rude Ranch continued to grow, the need to recruit volunteers became more important. Without volunteers, small non-profits like Rude Ranch could not survive. After all, two people could only accomplish so much by themselves before they went insane (some called it burn out). We were trying to avoid that special trip to the funny farm.

We were lucky to have a number of dedicated volunteers over the years. Many volunteers had come and gone, but a few stuck with us through thick and thin and became instrumental to our long-term success. Many of them were willing to step in and help when we really needed it. Most of them never even questioned our sanity.

Jill was one of the volunteers who proved this point. One night Bob received a call from Claire, one of our younger volunteers, and her mom. There was a Pygmy goat running around the high school parking lot. Could he help? Bob drove the three miles to the high school prepared to go into goat capture mode. No need. Claire and her mom had already rounded up the goat. Bob put the goat in the back of the Suburban and brought it back to Rude Ranch.

We were primarily set up as a cat sanctuary. Where was Bob planning to put a goat? The bathroom on the main floor was empty, so that room was now dubbed the "goat room." Now what would we feed it and give it for bedding? That was where Jill, our only volunteer with a horse, entered the picture.

I called Jill and asked if she could please bring some hay, sweet feed and straw over to Rude Ranch. She did exactly as requested without questioning me. I guess she knew there would be a reasonable explanation when she arrived.

Jill made the trip with the requested supplies and we completed the goat setup in the bathroom. Then Dr. Laura Martin arrived to give some of our kids their annual vaccinations. We thought as long as she was here, we'd let her give the goat a once over. She agreed that it was a Pygmy goat. Then it was time to figure out if it was a boy or a girl. Bob was elected for this delicate procedure and proclaimed "it's a girl." Then it was time to call it a night and get some much needed sleep.

When Bob went to check on the little goat in the morning, she was perched on a shelf that was mounted on the wall. I guess this was a Pygmy mountain goat. I was impressed that Bob installed a shelf that could actually hold a fifty pound goat. Then we got a call from Claire's mom. The police had been to her house in response to a flyer they put up about the goat. Someone had filed a stolen goat report two days earlier. It turned out the utility company was working in their yard and forgot to latch the gate behind them when they left. The goat took advantage of the situation and wandered off to explore the neighborhood. The family was both relieved and grateful to have their pet goat, Baby, back with them.

Goats Really Will Eat Anything

Jill, and many others, began volunteering with Rude Ranch over the past couple of years, but our first official volunteer was Joy. We first met her when we were all volunteering at the Save A Life shelter. When Bob and I started Rude Ranch she asked if we could use some help with our program. We didn't really know what our program was yet, but we knew Joy loved socializing cats and we had plenty of need for help with that activity. Joy started dropping by Rude Ranch every Saturday afternoon to spend time with the shy kids.

About ten years into her volunteer efforts, Joy finally decided it was time to adopt a Rude Ranch cat of her very own. It was a tough decision; by that time, we had more than 120 cats to choose from. She finally settled on Charity as the right choice for her and her feline family. After all, Joy had spent the last ten years helping to socialize her. It was one of those bittersweet moments for Bob and me. We had become very attached to Charity after ten years of caring for her, but we were thrilled she had finally found her forever home.

Barbara was another volunteer who had been with Rude Ranch for a long time. One day she called with a problem. A little cat showed up on her front porch and was limping pretty badly. Could we help with this little girl? Of course we would, and Barbara arrived shortly after that with the little cat. Bob gave her the once over, but couldn't find anything obvious to explain the limp. It was time to head to the vet.

Dr. Roller couldn't find anything obvious either. It must be from an old injury. A few minutes later, we had X-rays and discovered the cat's problem. She had been shot with a shotgun at some point. The X-rays showed her leg was shattered and there were still several pellets throughout her body. This tough little girl had survived a very serious injury on her very own.

Since she was doing well and everything had already healed, we thought the best course of action was to leave well enough alone. She would still need to be watched closely to see if there were any complications from the injury. Barbara and her husband Danny volunteered to foster her for a few weeks to monitor her progress. Soon after that they decided this little girl came to them for a reason and made her a permanent member of their family. She moved into their hearts and into their home and was now known as Ziva.

Shortly after that we had a new leukemia cat. Her name was Snowflake. She arrived via Dr. Bassford at the Four Legs Veterinary Hospital just down the road from us. She had been hit by a car and was suffering from injuries too numerous to mention. She was also incredibly sweet. We took her in and began the long process of treating her injuries. One thing that really helped this sweet little cat came from one of our younger volunteers.

Valerie and her eight year old daughter Cayleigh had just started volunteering when Snowflake arrived at Rude Ranch. They quickly bonded with this little sweetheart and Cayleigh decided to make her a little blanket of her own. Snowflake loved that blanket and curled up in it whenever she took a nap. Unfortunately, little Snowflake didn't survive her injuries, but she had lots of love from the volunteers and her little blanket to comfort her while she was with us.

Then Bob thought it was a good time to get sick. He'd been fighting a cold and sinus infection for some time. He was sick and tired of being sick and tired. I was getting tired of him being sick and tired. That meant one thing; he had to go to the doctor. Getting Bob to a doctor was like trying to keep a cat out of a room they shouldn't be in. The harder you tried to keep the cat out (or get Bob to a doctor) the more determined he was to do the opposite. I think it was a guy thing. Anyway, I finally took matters into my own hands and made him a 10:15 doctor's appointment for the next day.

On the day of the appointment, Bob arranged to meet his parents for breakfast near the doctor's office. I figured at least his mom would make sure he actually kept his doctor's appointment. Bob took the back roads to the restaurant. He always wanted to take the back roads everywhere. The route he took was the one that had a really creepy, one-lane bridge over the Patuxent River. That particular morning there was a traffic backup on both sides of the bridge. There were people standing around outside their cars, many of them talking on cell phones. Bob soon found out why traffic was at a stand still; there was a big goat standing in the middle of the bridge.

The goat was afraid to move and the people were afraid of the goat. Bob walked up to check things out (when you had a sign that said "animal rescue" on the side of your car, people expected you to deal with these types of things). Bob approached the goat to figure out what was wrong. People were freaking out, saying the goat was wild and would gore him. Bob noticed the goat was wearing a collar, which wasn't usually a fashion accessory worn by wild animals.

Once Bob reached the goat he found out why it wasn't moving. Its hooves were slipping through the steel grids on the bridge. The goat was afraid to move. That meant Bob had to carry the 150-pound goat off the bridge (did I mention it was pouring down rain and Bob and the goat were soaking wet by now)? It would have been smarter if Bob had the foresight to carry the goat to the side of the bridge where he parked the Suburban rather than the side closest to land. Now he had to turn around and carry the goat back across the bridge (I guess I had to cut him some slack on this one since he was sick).

Bob did make it to the other side of the bridge and loaded the goat in the back of the Suburban. Now it was time to figure out what to do with a wet, homeless goat. Then Bob caught a lucky break; one of the ladies who was stuck in the "Great Goat Backup" thought she recognized the goat. She had seen it in a yard about three miles away several times over the past few months.

Bob hopped into the Suburban armed with directions to the goats suspected home. He arrived at the house and discovered the front door was blocked by stacks of building materials. Being a somewhat intelligent male, he headed for the back door (seemed logical). Unfortunately for Bob, he was greeted by five Rottweilers that were hanging out on the back porch. There was a brief moment of panic as Bob did the calculations (did I mention Bob was a math major in college) and determined there was no way he could outrun five Rottweilers. He also determined he couldn't out-wrestle five Rottweilers. He took the do nothing approach and stood still (normally something I gave him a hard time about, but in this case, it was probably a wise decision). Then he noticed all five tails were wagging a happy wag and all they wanted was a little attention.

Bob took a brief moment to collect his thoughts, pet the dogs and decide if he needed to head home to change his shorts before knocking on the door. The goat was a family pet and had wandered off. With the goat safely back home, Bob headed out for his doctor's appointment. He just had to explain why he smelled like a wet goat.

The things a guy will do to try to get out of a doctor's appointment!

Tommy Visits the Emergency Vet

Most people don't understand Tommy, our eleventh cat (yes, Bob and I made Tommy a permanent resident). As you may remember from our earlier rescue adventures, Tommy had a checkered past. To be honest, if Tommy were human, he would be the leader of a biker gang, with several paternity suits, and a pack of cigarettes rolled up in his sleeve. To prove his tough guy image, Tommy frequently brawled with the other cats (and sometimes Bruno). Some ran from him, some took him on, and some, like Her Royal Highness Tia, would back him into a corner and smack him around.

Tommy could also be counted on for a couple of other things, but his love of food was his biggest weakness. If you ever wanted to find Tommy, just open a can of cat food and he would come running. That's why we knew something was wrong the night Tommy slept through dinner.

We tracked him down and he definitely did not look good. He was hot to the touch, as in a really high fever hot. By now Bob and I had acquired a little bit of knowledge about how to care for sick animals. We started by taking his temperature. It was 107.8, okay, that was really high.

We tried to give him some fluids to help cool him off and planned to follow that up with antibiotics for what was obviously some kind of infection. To say it didn't go well would be an understatement. As soon as we approached him with the needle, he started bucking like a bronco. It wasn't supposed to work like this: Whenever we went through this process with other sick cats, the cat quietly laid there like they were taking a sun bath. At the rate this guy was going, it would have been easier to get the needle into the mechanical bull from *Urban Cowboy*.

Bob and I felt we had no choice; Tommy was going to need more care than we could give him. So, we loaded him into a carrier and it was off to the emergency vet.

Fortunately, we had an in at the emergency vet. One of their vet techs also volunteered at Rude Ranch. She checked us in and soon an unsuspecting vet tech arrived to take Tommy, still in his carrier, back to the exam room. A few minutes later, the usual hubbub of the clinic was broken by loud caterwauling screams, followed by a few choice words of the human variety. We figured round one went to Tommy.

A few minutes later, the vet tech returned to the waiting room. She asked Bob if he would mind helping them get Tommy out of the carrier. Apparently he was putting up a pretty good fight. When Bob got to the treatment room, he witnessed two vet techs holding the carrier upside down and shaking it vigorously, with Tommy's hind legs hanging out. I guess Tommy wasn't as close to death as we thought. Bob took the carrier apart and a somewhat ticked-off Tommy was removed from its remains.

Then the vet arrived to see Tommy. The victim (vet) on duty that night was one who absolutely hated to sedate an animal unless absolutely necessary. The vet agreed Tommy had a really high fever, he just couldn't find a reason for it. Bob thought Tommy was limping a little on one of his front paws, so the vet stretched the paw out to look at it and Tommy promptly bit him. Then the vet thought he saw something on the other front paw and attempted to exam it. Tommy bit him again, a little harder this time since he didn't get his point across the first time. Then a statement was uttered that stunned even the vet techs: "Sir, would you mind if I sedated your cat before I examine him?"

Now that Tommy was well-sedated, they found several bite wounds on his leg from an apparent battle with one of the other Rude Cats.

About an hour and $300 later, Bob and a now sedated Tommy were on their way back home. It turned out we were right about the treatment for him, we just couldn't get Tommy to cooperate. We didn't feel all that bad after witnessing all the problems they had with Tommy at the emergency clinic. The vet did survive treating Tommy, but had a few impressive teeth marks as mementos of the occasion. We're not sure if Tommy had an influence on his decision, but we later heard the vet opened a catering business on the Eastern Shore of Maryland and left the veterinary profession. At least Tommy didn't get into any more trouble that night.

Now that Tommy was back to "normal," we started to contemplate the annual visit to the vet. The last one involved more adventure than we cared to experience again. Maybe it was time to have the vet come to Rude Ranch. We talked it over with Dr. Harrison, who wholeheartedly agreed.

Dr. Roller arrived for the first of many trips to Rude Ranch. We started with the easier animals and worked our way up to the feral room. They were never very cooperative for their exams, and we were usually lucky to get a quick once over and then update their vaccinations.

Our first foray into the feral room produced the expected results. All the cats headed for the hills with Quiver in the lead. Bob and I got our aerobic workout for the day as we flushed Quiver from under chairs, behind the table, under the shelves and from the top of the cat tree. Then Quiver made his first mistake. He jumped up on the top shelf in the closet. We had him cornered. Feeling victorious, Bob reached up and scruffed Quiver. Now that Bob had Quiver, we had a more immediate problem: Dr. Roller was a very petite woman, and Quiver was on the top shelf of the closet. I tried to smoothly slide a chair into position so Dr. Roller could reach Quiver's backside. Somehow Bob lost his balance during this process (Bob claimed I pushed him, but I was sticking with my story, it was an accident)! As Bob reached out to catch himself, Quiver reached out with all four canine teeth and buried them deep into Bob's forearm.

I got the distinct impression Bob was in a little bit of pain (maybe the numerous grunts and muffled curse words were a clue too). Dr. Roller was a little freaked out by the recent development. She was a vet, not a physician. Animal blood and body parts went with the territory, but human blood was another story altogether. Bob just yelled out, "Give the cat the shot and hurry." I guess he figured the cat was preoccupied with his forearm and wouldn't notice the needle in his backside. He was right.

Now that Quiver had gotten his rabies shot, it was time to deal with the pool of blood accumulating at Bob's feet. I was always complaining about cleaning up after Bob and this was no exception. He convinced us his need to care for his arm was far more important than cleaning up the mess he was leaving in his wake. I cut him a break this time and cleaned up his mess while he tended to his wounds.

In the end, Quiver survived the ordeal without any lasting psychological issues. Bob had four impressive holes in his arm that bled profusely all the way to the sink. He even grabbed my good dish towel as a temporary bandage (there were plenty of old towels, but he had to grab the only new one). Dr. Roller also survived her first session at Rude Ranch. It must not have been all that bad; she came back for many return engagements.

The Challenge of
Fundraising

One of the most important non animal aspects of running an animal sanctuary was having enough money to keep things operating; paying for food, medicines, vaccines and vet care to mention a few. Up until now, Bob and I were paying for everything out of our own pockets. Now that we were an official charity we could start asking for donations and raising funds. That was one of the tougher things for the average person to do, and we were no exception. One of the best pieces of advice we got was from Faith Maloney, one of the co-founders at the Best Friends Animal Sanctuary. She told us to not view it as raising money for ourselves, but to view it as raising money to help the animals. It did make it a little easier, but was still one of our most difficult tasks.

Usually the first fundraising idea that came to mind for most people was a bake sale! That was fine if you needed a couple hundred bucks and could bake. I was usually happy to produce a halfway edible dish that didn't have more than twenty cat hairs in it. We needed something bigger. By December of that year we had it: Photos with Santa!

If you've ever been near a PetSmart during those all important shopping weekends between Thanksgiving and Christmas, then you've probably seen the "Photos with Santa" spectacle. In the early years of this event you would get two Polaroid pictures of your pet posing with Santa. Santa, the elves and the photographer were provided by local animal shelters who received a portion of the proceeds from each photo package sold. The event worked well, the shelter could raise some money, people got to show off their pets and PetSmart made some extra money selling the items the pets stole off the shelves while waiting to have their pictures taken.

We jumped at the chance to do this, figuring it would be fun for our volunteers, a good way to raise much needed funds and a chance to do more adoptions (after all, while people waited in line for their picture, they'd be walking right past our animals). We started by recruiting volunteers: we had Claire and Andrea, twelve and fourteen years old respectively, who would be great as elves. We had several people to take pictures. Bob was a somewhat unwilling natural for Santa. We advertised the event like nobody's business, and we had an action plan for the entire event. We were ready to roll.

On the first day of Bob's debut as Santa, he left early in the two-seater sports car with his elf, Claire. They barely made it two miles when they saw two German Short Haired Pointers running along the side of the road. A car was stopped near the dogs and a lady was trying to coax them over to her. Bob (Santa) couldn't resist and pulled off to the side of the road. I guess the dogs heard about the good things that followed if you were nice to Santa and came right over to him. Of course that created a small dilemma; Santa and Claire were in a small car and these were two rather large dogs. Also, Santa had a date with a lot of other animals in the not too distant future. Fortunately, the lady who pulled off to the side of the road was also an animal lover and agreed to take the dogs home with her and try to find their parents. Santa was back on his journey to PetSmart.

Bob and Claire arrived safely at the PetSmart. They did get some interesting looks along the way. I guess most people expected Santa to be driving a sleigh with reindeer, not cruising down the road in a sports car. I followed later driving the Suburban with the cats that were up for adoption.

Soon the fun began. Bob's first photo was with a calm dog, no sweat. Then a Yorkie puppy arrived, which would have been fine, except it got lost in Santa's beard. Then a full sized Great Dane reached the front of the line. Who would have thought a Great Dane would be afraid of Santa? The dog took off, but at least he stopped running somewhere in the warehouse at the back of the store. Then we were surprised how much liquid a Miniature Dachshund could produce while peeing on Santa's leg. At least it wasn't the Bull Mastiff that was next in line. That's when we learned Bull Mastiff's pretty much needed an entire aisle to themselves and had to be coerced into posing with Santa. It didn't go too well when Santa tried to lift the 200 pound dog onto the bench. I had never seen Santa with a hernia before and I didn't want to start now. We finally settled on Santa kneeling next to the dog and got a pretty good picture that way.

Then we discovered why you should always have a cat on a harness and leash rather than just perched on your shoulder when out in public. As soon as the cat saw all the dogs, it launched itself to the highest point it could reach. At least Santa was tall enough to retrieve the cat from the top shelf and return him to his parents. The cat did pose nicely for its picture once they made it to the front of the line. We also discovered the Santa suit was really hot (or at least that was what Bob claimed). This was especially true when Santa spent the entire day wrestling with a lot of hot, furry bodies.

All in all, it was a very successful event over the years. We consistently raised more money than most groups doing this type of fundraiser. We owed that to the tremendous support from the local media, like the *Annapolis Capital,* and all our volunteers and adoptive parents. I think the only one who didn't appreciate the huge turnouts was Bob. He equated the Santa suit to sitting in a hot sauna all day with a wet dog; although, he still had a blast "playing" with all the animals. We even had a baby monkey stop by for a photo once. The poor little thing was terrified of Santa, but still posed for some great pictures.

Santa Bob Doing his Tarzan Impersonation

Over the years we moved on to other fundraisers; basket bingo, yard sales, and flyer mail-outs. Still the fundraiser everyone, with the possible exception of Bob, enjoyed the most was Photos with Santa.

Being government employees, or ex-employees in Bob's case, we were also aware of a few other fundraising avenues, mainly the government's Combined Federal Campaign or CFC as it was known. This program allowed federal employees to donate to charities through payroll deduction. We were lucky that our Washington D.C. area had the highest concentration of federal employees in the world. We also knew a lot of federal employees and were hoping they would support our cause. If we could figure out the paperwork, this could be huge.

We started by calling the Office of Personnel Management, the group in charge of the program. We asked all kinds of questions and were given assurances we would qualify for the program. We sent our application and supporting paperwork in well before the deadline. We heard nothing. We called back. Our application wasn't in the stack. We were told it must have been lost in the mail. We had sent it certified mail. A quick call to the post office and we had the name of the person who signed for it. Guess who? Yep, the person who said they didn't receive it.

We called back with this information. She changed her story; it was thrown away as unqualified. "Why?" we asked. "It's because you filled out the paperwork wrong. You have to apply differently because you are a very small group." "Why weren't we told this when we called?" we asked the nice lady who originally told us how to apply. "You didn't ask," she said.

It turned out there were different forms for small, local groups. They had to apply individually to all the local CFC agencies. If we were a large, national group, we could just apply once for the entire country. At least we now knew the right questions to ask. Although we missed the deadline for that year, we were ready to do battle the next year. This time we got our information from a charity that had experience with CFC and got everything right. I think I now remembered why Bob left the federal government to do animal rescue in the first place.

Surviving the Hard Times

During the summer of 2002, we had our first crisis at Rude Ranch: panleukopenia, better known as feline distemper. Up to now we were very lucky and blissfully ignorant regarding some of the deadly viruses that could invade an animal sanctuary. We weren't sure exactly where it originated, but we had several kittens showing signs of the illness. We had just taken in thirty kittens, eighteen from an animal control in West Virginia and twelve from an animal control on Maryland's Eastern Shore.

The first signs of the illness appeared in two of the kittens; one from West Virginia and one from the Eastern Shore. Within hours both kittens started vomiting, had bloody diarrhea, and high fevers. At first we thought it was a combination of new food, deworming medicine and vaccines. But then both kittens went down hill quickly overnight.

We realized we were in over our heads and rushed the kittens to the emergency vet. They told us there was little they could do; the kittens had distemper and there was no effective treatment for the disease. They started them on IV fluids and antibiotics. Basic supportive therapy was all they could do we were told. The rest was up to the kittens. They told us we would probably lose all the kittens at the sanctuary and most likely many of the other animals as this was a highly contagious, deadly disease. These weren't the words of advice we were hoping to hear.

Several hours of frenzied research later, we knew we needed a game plan and quick. Feline distemper was an often deadly, easily transmitted virus that would strike unvaccinated cats and kittens. The virus destroyed the lining of the intestines, meaning the cat's body couldn't absorb nutrients. When faced with a diagnosis of distemper, most vets predicted such a small chance of survival that euthanasia was automatically recommended. The vet at the emergency clinic went on to recommend euthanizing every kitten at the sanctuary, even ones that weren't exhibiting symptoms and weren't directly exposed to the virus.

While we didn't want the kittens to suffer, we were having a lot of trouble buying into a mass "culling" of our animals; especially the ones that showed no signs of the illness. Fortunately, we tracked down an infectious disease vet who gave us some hope. She pointed us to newer research and experimental treatments.

We spent the next few weeks learning more about distemper than we had ever wanted to know. We were now providing twenty-four hour critical care to all the kittens. Each kitten was given fluids, antiviral medicine, antibiotics and fed a special mixture of food and nutritional supplements every four hours.

They were weighed twice a day to monitor their condition and make adjustments to their treatments. To prevent further cross contamination, each kitten was separated from its litter mates and kept in its own area. The theory was if we could keep them alive through the first ten days and prevent pneumonia from developing, the kittens would have a pretty good chance of making it.

To keep up with this schedule, Bob and I took turns for the 3 a.m. feedings. About two weeks into the treatments, Bob fell asleep on the floor during a midnight feeding. I thought about waking him up, but it seemed kind of silly to wake him up just to go to bed. At least he was already there for the next feeding. (I think it was my turn, but oh well!)

That was definitely a dark time at Rude Ranch, made worse by the many summer thunderstorms we had, knocking out our electricity. Many times we fed and weighed the kittens by flashlight. Maybe investing in a generator would be a good idea.

About eighteen days after the first signs of illness, we started to notice some of the kittens were starting to look a little brighter. They seemed a little more active, and were gaining weight. A few days later we could definitely see improvements. The kittens were getting rowdy and starting to play. One enterprising kitten even figured out how to manipulate the cage dividers and broke into his brother's cage. We were able to cut out the middle-of-the-night feedings and wean the kittens off their medications.

Unfortunately, we lost eleven of the thirty kittens. Five of the kittens succumbed to the distemper virus, and the remaining six kittens to pneumonia. The nineteen surviving kittens were healthy and showed no lasting affects of their illness. Although exhausted, Bob and I were glad we saved as many as we did. We owed a huge debt of gratitude to Dr. Darden, the vet who offered us her expert advice on the treatment for distemper.

Vacationing with Marilyn

By August 2002, Bob and I decided things at the sanctuary were stable enough we could "vacation" for a few days. At this point we had 115 cats, three dogs and an unknown number of fish at the sanctuary. It wasn't exactly a normal pet sitter job. This would require a scheduling and coordination effort of epic proportions. We started ten weeks ahead of time: lined up our anchor people, scheduled the volunteers, and had veterinarians on standby. We were loading all the data into a Microsoft spread sheet to help organize our vacation. We almost blew up the printer trying to print enough copies for everyone.

Eventually we had the schedule nailed down, the check lists written, emergency phone numbers distributed and travel plans made. Then we told people where we were going. That was when everyone really started questioning our sanity. We were going to Best Friends Animal Sanctuary in Kanab, Utah. That's right; we were going to spend our vacation at another animal sanctuary!

For those of you who haven't heard of Best Friends, it is one of the largest and most impressive animal sanctuaries in the country. We were making the trip as a vacation, but also to see how a major, established sanctuary functioned and to see if we could pick up any pointers. In return, we would help care for the animals and attempt to make ourselves useful.

Bob and Kathy at Best Friends

On the day of our departure, Bob and I woke up at 4 a.m. We wanted to allow enough time to make our 8 a.m. flight. We did a final check on all the kids. All was going well until we entered the general population room. We noticed a blast of warm humid air as soon as we opened the door. Then we noticed that a window was open in the room, and of course the screen was punched out. This was something you didn't want to find at 4 a.m. when you were leaving to catch an 8 a.m. flight. We did a quick paw and tail count and fortunately, no one was missing.

Apparently, the cats liked the air conditioned room with pillows and a twenty-four hour buffet more than an adventure in the hot, humid outside world. We knew the culprit who opened the window had to be Oscar, a new cat that had been playing with the window latches the day before. Now our problem was how to secure the window so he wouldn't get it open while we were gone. It was amazing what you could do with duct tape.

Now that we had the window secured and everyone accounted for, we left for the airport. We picked up Alexis on the way; she was a Rude Ranch volunteer who had been to Best Friends before and had offered to be our tour guide. We even managed to make it to the airport on-time after our morning adventures. The flight took off on-time and landed a few hours later in Las Vegas, the closest major airport to Best Friends. Our next step was to pick up the rental car and head northeast towards Utah.

That was where I ran into a little trouble. Somehow I ended up driving, which was fine, except Bob and Alexis had fallen asleep and the directions were in the back with Alexis. I winged it and kept following the signs to Utah.

We eventually arrived at Best Friends, and checked into our cabin. We spent the first day getting the lay of the land, taking the volunteer tour and meeting the people we would be working with the rest of the week. We found out Best Friends was founded in the early 1980's by about thirty people who all had a desire to help animals. Their property was nestled in a place called Angel Canyon and consisted of thousands of acres of beautiful high desert plateaus with great views of red rock cliffs and the mountains of southern Utah on the horizon.

On our second day we met Marilyn. She was a Snowshoe Siamese living in Benton's House, one of the special needs cat buildings at the sanctuary. Her mother had suffered from distemper while she was pregnant. As a result, Marilyn was born with neurological damage that made it difficult for her to control her legs. She walked a little like a sailor might walk after a weekend of liberty.

While we were in Benton's House, Marilyn started following us around. When we went into a room and came out she would be there waiting for us. When Bob sat down in a chair, she crawled into his lap and fell asleep. This cat was clearly working us. We started thinking about Marilyn; after all, we needed a twelfth Rude Cat like we needed a lobotomy. But she didn't follow anyone else around the building, even the sanctuary staffers. After some prompting from Alexis and me, Bob decided to see if we could adopt her.

Marilyn Relaxing after Arriving at Rude Ranch

Vivian, one of the co-founders of Best Friends, was the only person around that day who worked on cat adoptions. Bob and I went to her office to discuss adopting Marilyn. That was when we found out a few more details about Marilyn. She wasn't a good shot at the litter box. While that would slow down most people during the adoption process, we already had Tommy, the king of the sprayers in the house. We figured as long as Marilyn was consistent where she missed, we wouldn't have a problem. That pretty much clinched it. Now we had to figure out how to get Ms. Marilyn back home.

The main problem was scheduling a flight. We were leaving the next day and the airline we were using didn't have space for a cat on our flight. We talked this over with Vivian and decided Bob would fly back at a later date to get Marilyn. They would be happy to hold onto her until we could make arrangements to pick her up.

Eventually all the details were worked out; Bob would fly to Las Vegas (poor thing), meet representatives from Best Friends at a local PetSmart, and pick up Marilyn. Their vet would provide a sedative to give her for the five-hour plane flight back to Maryland. It seemed simple enough.

When the day arrived, Bob dutifully left for the airport three hours before his noon flight. He parked the car, made it through the security check points and to the gate without any problem. Then he waited, and waited. It turned out the plane wasn't going to take off; it was pulled out of service for mechanical problems. Luckily he was re-booked on another flight an hour later. Okay, a little delay, but not horrible.

By 8 p.m. that night I figured Bob had pretty much made his way to Vegas. That was when I got a call from Philadelphia: The flight Bob was re-booked on was also cancelled. He was put on still another flight. That flight also developed problems and was diverted to Philadelphia. It seemed to me that this route was the long way to get there.

Bob eventually made it to Vegas, picked up his rental car and made it to the PetSmart in time to pick up Marilyn. Once he got there, it turned out Best Friends was short of people for their adoption event. Could Bob help out? He didn't have anywhere else to be for a few hours so why not. Bob and Marilyn helped out with adoptions for a few hours and then made their way to the airport. That probably saved us some money in the long run. Considering Bob's luck with the planes, he probably would have lost a lot of money on the slot machines if he had arrived early.

Once they arrived at the airport, they made it through security and arrived at the boarding gate with plenty of time to spare. While Bob and Marilyn were waiting for the plane, a nice couple started talking to Bob and ended up making a donation to help with our rescue work.

Then it was getting close to boarding time, so Bob dutifully gave Marilyn her sedative. Rather than calming Marilyn down, it had the opposite affect. Then the flight took off, and so did Marilyn. She didn't stop screaming until they landed in Maryland. At one point Bob thought he would have to use the donation to buy a round of drinks for everyone on the plane or risk being thrown into the cargo hold.

They finally made it home around 3 a.m. Although it took a little while for her to settle in, Marilyn took her new role as our special needs mascot very seriously.

The Great Blizzard of 2003

I remembered someone once commenting that about every five years the Maryland area really gets "whomped" with snow. From my experience, that was reasonably accurate. I remembered fearfully driving home from work in my little Pontiac Sunbird during the Veterans Day storm in 1986. There was some kind of work-closing storm (the best kind) around 1991. I remembered that storm distinctly as Bob, his parents and his sisters were all laughing at the entire region for shutting down because of a little bit of snow (Wisconsin humor I guess). I definitely remembered the double blast of snow in 1996; even the weather forecasters apologized for screwing that one up. Bob and I built a huge kitty condo during that one. Then there was the storm that wasn't supposed to happen in 2001. That was when the forecasters predicted light sleet and we ended up with nineteen inches of snow. It was during that storm that Bob and I hatched the basic ground work for starting Rude Ranch. Judging from our history, we would really have to do something big during the next snowstorm. However, with the big snow of 2001 out of the way, we thought we had a couple of years.

That was why in February of 2003, when the weather forecasters first started predicting a "major snow event," we were wary. After all, it was totally off schedule. We weren't due for a major snowfall for another three years. As the week wore on we started to see signs that everyone else thought we were in for some serious snow. So, like everyone else, we started checking our supplies: kitty litter, cat food, dog food, chocolate chips, and our main staple, diet soda (okay, maybe it wasn't just like everyone else. We didn't worry as much about the bread, milk and toilet paper). We also brought most of our firewood into the house thinking it would be nice to have a roaring fire while the snow fell. We were really hoping the Rude Cats wouldn't pee on the firewood before it went into the fireplace.

Despite our preparations, we did have a couple of pressing issues: the storm was scheduled to hit on a Saturday, our major PetSmart adoption day. We also had people driving down from New York to pick up a cat and they planned to drive back the same day.

By Friday evening the weather forecasters were predicting "end of the world" type stuff: sleet, hail, freezing rain, snow, back to sleet and freezing rain, then snow, and more snow. In terms of our adoption event, the people from the north were thinking it would be fun, but the people that weren't used to driving in the snow were freaking out. So, being the extremely decisive types, we "played it by ear."

The next morning dawned bright and sunny. The weather forecasters were still predicting dire consequences for anyone daring to venture out. We cancelled the adoption event much to everyone's relief. We took care of the cats, let the dogs out to play in the yard, and settled in for the long haul. The people picking up the New York bound cat arrived, snickering about all the hoopla over the "storm" (but we did notice they arrived about two hours ahead of their appointment, and left rather quickly after we finalized the adoption).

Soon a light snow started to fall. It was pretty. The dogs were having a good time rolling around in it. It sure didn't seem like the heavy stuff we were told was on the way. By the end of the night we still had some snow falling, but it was nowhere near what we were told to expect. The weather forecasters kept saying "just wait." Through it all, Bones and Marilyn, our mascots, worked hard (napping the day away).

Bones and Marilyn Hard at Work

The next day we woke up to about six inches of snow on the ground. It was beautiful. It was still falling. The weather forecasters were still predicting a lot of snow. We knew we would be on our own taking care of the animals that day. People in this area rarely ventured out when it was snowing like this. Throughout the day, the snow kept falling. By 2 p.m. we had about fourteen inches of snow. The dogs gave up and were sleeping by the fire. By now it was a more "keep on falling so work will be closed tomorrow" kind of feeling. At 6 p.m., we had about twenty inches of snow and I got my wish. The message most federal employees hoped to hear: "the federal government offices would be closed on Monday." By the time all was said and done, we had a lot of snow.

After three days we were still trying to figure out which "lumps" in the snow were cars and which ones were bushes.

We tried to let the dogs out by opening the garage door but the snow had drifted up against the door and it looked like a five foot wall of white had appeared overnight. Boomer, the little guy, gave up, pee'd on the lawn mower and snuggled up in his blanket in front of the heater. Ceasar and Bruno went out in the snow and jumped through it like deer. They were having a blast running around like two little kids. Bruno had finally found a temperature that fit his breeding.

Then Ceasar did his "king of the hill" routine and perched on top of a snow bank. It was great until the snow collapsed under him and he went straight down. He dug his way out, came running back to the garage like his tail was on fire, then turned around and starting barking at the snow. I guess he figured barking at the snow showed it who was boss.

Now we had to figure out a few more things. We knew the newspaper was pretty much a goner for the week. We also figured that maybe we really should have spent the money for the snow plow. Fortunately, the main road would be plowed out soon. That was one of the perks of living on a snow emergency route; the roads were plowed quickly and the trash would be picked up. It would just be a matter of getting the trash out to the street (let's face it; we generated a lot of trash with 120 plus animals)!

After a couple of days, the snow started to melt away. We dug a path to the front door for the people coming and going. The snow eventually got a crust on top that Boomer and Ceasar could walk across without falling through. This was a development that irritated Bruno as he would try to run across the yard under a full head of steam, then suddenly "fall through" and end up doing a face plant in the snow. At least he didn't feel the need to bark at the snow.

Now that the winter storm was over, life at Rude Ranch was back to our semi-normal existence and we even managed to avoid doing anything crazy during the storm, like starting an animal sanctuary.

The winter was starting to turn into a rainy spring. Things were fairly calm, and then we awoke to the sound of our phone ringing repeatedly around 4:30 one morning. Usually it took the sound of a cat hacking a hairball on the bed to get us moving that early. It turned out the calls were from Alexis, one of our volunteers. She needed help. She had just found a five week old kitten flopping around in the woods behind her house. She couldn't leave the helpless kitten in the woods, but she had to go to work. Could she bring it to us for the day?

It wasn't long before she arrived with a very damp, very frizzy ball of fluff. Despite his frizziness we had to admit the little guy was incredibly adorable, with a cute little wobble that was very endearing. We were a little concerned about his shaking and wobbling, especially his eating. Unless we held his head over the food, he bobbed and wobbled so much he couldn't line his mouth up with the food. His attempts to drink water didn't go much better. At least he managed to "flop" into and out of the litter box. It didn't take us long to come up with a diagnosis: cerebellular hyperplasia, the same thing afflicting our special needs mascot, Marilyn.

Beanie, Our Little Neurological Cutie

At least this guy, unlike Marilyn, was a good shot at the litter box. Although we couldn't cure the hyperplasia, we could do a lot of physical therapy to help build up his muscles and improve his coordination.

The little guy, now called Beanie, eventually learned to eat without having his head held. He even learned to run and play like any other cat. The only difference was that every now and then his back end would get ahead of his front end and he would turn into a big rolling ball of fur and legs. Andrea, a regular Rude Ranch volunteer, and her family fell in love with the little cutie and took him home to live with them.

Just as Beanie was getting stronger and moving into his new home, we found ourselves in another situation we never dreamed would happen to us; we became the victims of identity theft by an animal hoarder. We started getting suspicious when we received several calls and emails from various shelters asking us for proof of rabies or to send them spay/neuter certificates for an animal we took from them. That was standard procedure for most animal control agencies when they released animals to other groups. The only problem was these requests were for animals that never came to us. Some of the requests were coming from shelters as far away as Florida. Unless Bob was sneaking away for vacations while I was asleep, I was pretty sure we hadn't been to Florida recently.

At first we chalked it up to record-keeping errors. Then during the height of kitten season it all blew apart. We got an email from one of Maryland's Eastern Shore animal controls thanking us for taking fifty kittens the previous week. We sent back "what fifty kittens?" It took a little investigating but we found out a former volunteer we knew from our Save A Life days was using the name of Rude Ranch and Save A Life to collect animals from various shelters all over the east coast. With our help, the State's Attorney's office and the local animal control agency started an investigation. It took several months for them to build a case, but they still couldn't get approval for a search warrant. Then the investigators finally caught a break; the hoarder rented a house in the same county and essentially destroyed it. They had more than eighty cats and dogs living in the house and hadn't been keeping up with their care. The landlord wanted to press charges and attempt to recover his losses. Using evidence from the rental property, the authorities could go for felony animal abuse charges and get a search warrant to enter the hoarder's other property.

The day of the seizure was filled with tension and apprehension. The animal control director asked us if we could take some of their existing animals. They knew they would need to make room for the animals that they assumed would be seized the next day. We made the one hour drive and brought back about twenty cats and kittens. Then we were invited to participate in the raid itself and help sort out the mess they expected to find there. We couldn't work that into our schedule, but offered to help where we could after the raid. They weren't sure how many animals to expect, but based on information from us and other groups, they knew it would be a lot.

The animal control agency removed 485 cats and dogs from the house the next day. Many were in bad shape and all had to be held as evidence. We went back to their shelter and took over sixty cats and kittens over a forty-eight hour period. That included a few last minute additions, like a mom and six kittens that were handed over to Bob in the parking lot. As Bob carried the feline family to the car, a little girl ran over and started kicking Bob in the shins, screaming that he was taking her pet. To preserve his legs, Bob pointed out that he was saving her cat and kittens; it was her mommy that was getting rid of them. I don't think the mom appreciated that, but Bob was taking a beating and the mom was doing nothing to stop the child.

In the end, the animal hoarder took an Alfred plea, meaning she wouldn't admit guilt, but knew there was enough evidence to convict her. She and her husband got three years probation and court-ordered psychiatric counseling. It took months to untangle the paperwork among the assorted shelters and agencies that were deceived. Bob's bruises from his "kicking incident" finally faded, but he still flinches whenever he sees a four year old child.

We always try to look for the positive aspects in any situation. This case made it very difficult, but one good thing did come out of this horrible situation for Rude Ranch. It involved one of the kittens we pulled from the animal control agency. She was a cute little torti kitten we named Tabitha. Ken, the gentleman who adopted her, noticed all the animals we had at Rude Ranch. He asked how we managed to care for them and if we ever needed any help. We had become pretty good at jumping on any opportunity for help and quickly told Ken we could always use another volunteer. He only lived a few miles away, was retired and had some free time. Ken started volunteering the next week and has been with us ever since.

Hurricane Isabel

When Hurricane Isabel rolled around in October of 2003 we thought we were prepared. We had candles, food, and firewood stacked up. We had hoped to have the backup generator in place and ready to go, but unfortunately it hadn't arrived yet. The day before the Hurricane, we hurriedly stuffed outside equipment under the deck and "battened down the hatches." Our only concern was the Pip Squeak, a little four week old undersized orphaned kitten that needed to be fed every three hours and kept warm.

As a side note, the Pip Squeak was the model for the cover of this book. She looks cute and innocent in the picture, but she does have her feisty side and many of our volunteers have learned to have a fearful respect for her. Now back to the Hurricane.

The morning of the Hurricane started out rainy, but not too bad. We had twelve cats and kittens scheduled for spay/neuter surgeries. We checked at the vet clinic to make sure everything was still running normally. The vets were willing to do the surgeries so we dropped the cats off at the clinic, returned home and settled in to wait for the storm. The wind picked up by mid-afternoon; right about that time the dogs got really bored and wanted to go out and play. The weather wasn't all that bad yet, so we allowed them one more play and bathroom session before things got worse.

The vet clinic called and said all the surgeries were done, but if we wanted they could hold the cats for us overnight because of the storm.

We decided that was a good deal; it was around four o'clock and the winds were gusting at fifty miles per hour.

Then things got really bad. The cable went out. That could be a serious problem if your favorite show was about to start. About an hour later the power went out. That's when we regretted not starting on the generator project a little earlier.

We made it through the night unscathed, although we could hear the wind and rain blowing like crazy through the trees. By morning things were much calmer and it appeared most of the damage was relatively minor. It mainly consisted of a few tree limbs in the yard and one of the neighbor's big trees had fallen down across our road. That meant anyone trying to get out of our little neighborhood would have to take a short detour through our yard. Not really a problem; nobody seemed anxious to go out yet anyway.

Without electricity, our main concern was keeping the Pip Squeak warm. We didn't have the option of "nuking" a water bottle for her, so we started up the car and put the heater on full blast with the kitten under the vent. At least she seemed to enjoy the blow dryer effect.

Once the Pip Squeak was fed and snuggled in her bed, we set off to pick up the cats that had spent the night at the vet clinic. We got out of our neighborhood without too much trouble, but getting to the main road made us feel like the proverbial mouse in a maze. There were trees and power lines down all over the area. We slowly worked our way toward the clinic, trying one alternate route after another, until we got to the "Creepy Bridge."

This bridge was a narrow, spooky, one-lane bridge over the Patuxent River in the middle of dark, spooky woods. Local legend called it the Goatman Bridge. We just called it the Creepy Bridge. This was the same bridge where Bob rescued the goat a couple of years ago. Maybe there was something to the name.

The problem with the Creepy Bridge was not that the bridge itself flooded, but that the road at the end of the bridge flooded after any light rain. Hurricane Isabel certainly dropped more than that. Sure enough, although the bridge itself was above water, most of the road on the other side wasn't. While Bob had driven through the flooded area many times in the past, this time it looked much deeper than normal.

I was about to voice (yell!!!) my concern about this when Bob decided to "go for it" and floored it.

We made it about twenty feet before the water started coming into the Suburban through the air vents. Momentum got us maybe another five feet. At that point it wasn't looking like we would make it the rest of the way across the river. As bleak as things looked, we figured at least we weren't floating down the river. Then it happened, our 5,000 pound, heavyweight Chevy Suburban started floating sideways.

The Creepy Bridge Over the Patuxent River

Now Bob was one of those analytical types who liked to think a problem to death before taking action. The water inside the Suburban was now up to the seats. Bob decided to forego the analytical approach and take action. He jumped out of the Suburban through the window into chest deep water and started to "push" it the rest of the way across the river. He yelled at me to move over and grab the steering wheel.

From what I could recall in the few seconds before we turned the Suburban into a boat, there was no James Bond rudder-like attachment to steer the Suburban through the water. At least Bob was able to stop the downstream momentum of the car before he ran out of energy. I was just sitting in a pool of water wondering what to do next. To Bob's credit, he eventually pushed the Suburban far enough up the road that the front wheels touched down on solid ground. Maybe there was an advantage to being married to a guy that weighed over 300 pounds and used to be into weight lifting.

Just as Bob got all four tires on semi-solid ground, a couple of guys with pick-up trucks showed up on our side of the river. They ventured down to the river to see how high the water was and to see if any idiots had tried to make it across. We were able to deal with them laughing at us a lot better when they offered to pull us onto dryer land. Bob just had to wade to the front of the Suburban and hook it up (at least the bumper didn't fly off when they started pulling).

Once the Suburban was out of the water, we opened the doors and watched "the gusher" of water drain out of the vehicle. About that time, my cell phone rang. It was Alexis checking to see how we were doing after the storm. Once I told her what happened, she hopped in her car and made the twenty minute drive to us, relishing in the opportunity to give Bob a hard time. She also brought along a digital camera to document the adventure for posterity and future blackmail opportunities.

As Alexis and I were discussing the situation, she started swatting at a bug flying around her car. It was a bee and it promptly stung her. That was when we found out Alexis was severely allergic to bee stings. It would have been really helpful if she had an epi-pen with her. We rearranged our priorities a little bit. I took Alexis to the hospital and Bob worked on getting the Suburban running with the help of his new guy friends. Apparently submerging the engine in water hadn't done it much good. At least Bob knew enough to turn off the engine once we started floating.

Like most of the area, the hospital had also lost power, but was running on generators. Fortunately, bee sting allergies were considered pretty serious, so the nurse took Alexis straight back to an exam room. By now it had been close to three hours since the Pip Squeak had been fed and warmed up. With no word from Bob, I figured I was the most likely candidate to make my way back to the ranch for orphan duty.

I sent a note back to the treatment area to let Alexis know I would be back soon and headed towards home.

Apparently a few more trees had fallen while we were gone. After two detours and a trip through the next county south of us, I finally made it back to find the Pip Squeak snuggled in her blankie and waiting for lunch. By then Bob checked in to report the Suburban was running. He was making his way to pick up the cats at the clinic (remember, that's the reason we headed out to begin with). I was heading back to the hospital to pick up Alexis.

Alexis was given a shot of Benedryl and released from the hospital while I was back at the sanctuary. That would have been fine, except she decided to start walking toward the main street to meet me. Unfortunately, the Benedryl made her woozy enough that she went the wrong way. By the time I had figured out what happened, she had walked quite a distance into the surrounding neighborhood. I finally tracked her down and now with everyone located and heading back towards the ranch, we moved on to the next problem. Lunch for the humans. Bob had worked up a hunger pushing the Suburban across the river, and now he expected us to feed him. We dug up some leftovers that tasted pretty good cold and called it good enough.

It was now 2:30 in the afternoon and we hadn't even started cleaning up after the animals. Alexis was feeling a little better and offered to give us a hand with the fun of scooping litter boxes, changing the water and feeding the critters. It was a little challenging scooping litter boxes by flashlight, but we eventually finished the job. It wasn't our best job of cleaning, but under the circumstances nobody was complaining. The cats were just happy to get their afternoon meal of wet food a few hours late.

The power was restored in about four days. We realized the power was back when all the overhead lights came on at 3:00 a.m. and almost blinded us. The cable came back on a few hours later. The Suburban took three weeks to totally dry out, and never did run the same again. Overall, we survived Hurricane Isabel with relatively few problems. However, the next time Bob even thought about driving through anything bigger than a mud puddle, he would have to answer to me and my rolling pin (what the heck, I'd throw in the frying pan too).

Help Wanted, Please!!!

The days following Hurricane Isabel passed quickly as we were busy running adoption events, caring for the animals, doing the paperwork, and keeping up a full fundraising schedule. Bob and I were putting in close to twenty hours a day and were still falling behind. We had many loyal volunteers who helped on weekends, but most worked during the week. We needed help (physical help, the mental part was already a lost cause).

We checked and rechecked the budget. As long as we could keep Boomer from destroying the cat toys, no one ended up at the emergency vet and the dogs cut down on pig ears, we could afford to hire a part-time caretaker. We realized that would open a can of worms administratively, but at the same time, we figured Bob and I would make a better impression representing Rude Ranch if we weren't yawning and picking kitty litter out of our nails.

Being on a tight budget, we started by posting "Help Wanted" flyers on bulletin boards at local businesses and libraries. In response to the flyers, thirty-two people called to give up animals. One person asked if we could help find her peacock. Another lady said she would take the job, but would have to bring her three kids with her. None of this was exactly what we were looking for when we posted the flyer. Finally, we broke down and paid to run an ad in the local classified section. The gist of the ad said: "Wanted: part-time animal caretaker to help care for cats in a no-kill animal sanctuary." It seemed pretty straightforward to us.

One interviewee was afraid of cats. Another was "meant to care for animals" but was totally grossed out by poop, snot, and vomit, so she couldn't do anything with any of that stuff. One young lady showed up wearing a $300 suit and perfectly manicured nails. She didn't even make it through the door (this wasn't exactly a dry-clean only lifestyle).

Several times we thought we had found someone, offered them the job and they kind of forgot to show up on the first day. One young lady lasted twenty minutes before she remembered an important doctor's appointment and was never seen again.

Finally we found Suzanne. She lived up the street from us and was looking for a part-time job. She had four cats of her own and had volunteered at other animal shelters in the past. More importantly, the cats seemed to like her. Even Xander, the really shy boy greeted her. Figuring she had the approval of the "real people in charge," the Rude Cats, we hired her.

Suzanne helped care for the animals for several years before moving on. By then Andrea and Amber, two of our younger volunteers, were old enough to purchase and drive cars. That would have been inconsequential to Rude Ranch except the new drivers needed gas money for the cars. We figured they already knew how to scoop litter boxes and knew all the cats, so they hired on after Suzanne left.

By now, the administrative side of Rude Ranch was consuming more and more of my time. We needed to hire an administrative person so I could spend more time focusing on the fundraising. The person for this job would need one important skill in addition to the normal administrative duties. This person would have to deal with the combined flakiness of Bob and me. After all, we decided to start an animal sanctuary without having our heads examined.

Fortunately, we found Sue Ann. She had been volunteering with us for a couple of years, helping with mail-outs, and writing thank you notes. She and her husband Bob had three cats of their own so she was used to having feline assistants. Sue Ann signed on with us and has kept Bob and me in line ever since.

The next decision we made was one of the biggest of our lives. I would leave my job at the Census Bureau, our last vestige of steady income, and start working full-time promoting Rude Ranch and hopefully expand our programs to help more animals. We crunched the numbers up one side and down the other. It appeared we could make ends meet and make that final step to dedicate all our time to helping animals.

I was having a really difficult time with the decision, but Bob finally convinced me to take the plunge. "You only live once and have to decide what is most important in life" he told me. For us, it was helping animals (maybe we were certifiable).

I put in my notice and crossed all my fingers and toes that our investments would hold out and I would be able to increase our fundraising efforts to cover the cost of caring for the animals.

It's Kitten Season

The winter holidays came and went before we knew it. We were now coming into what was known in the animal rescue world as "Kitten Season." It usually started around the end of March, just as the days were getting longer and the first spring flowers started popping out. Likewise, this was when many kittens started to "pop out," often in barns, under sheds, behind porches and in garages. We were getting accustomed to panic-induced calls from all over asking for help. One call in particular caught our attention. A horse trainer from the local race horse training track had two litters of kittens in one of the barns. Could we help?

These particular kittens were born in one of the horse stables. Now they were sick with bad eyes and horrible colds. The track vet tried to treat the kittens, but his expertise was in horses, not cats. The horse trainer wanted to help the kittens, but felt she was in over her head and needed help.

Thinking the kittens probably needed a few days of antibiotic treatment to get over their illness, we agreed to take them. It wasn't until the kittens arrived that we realized we were also in over our heads; way over our heads. The kittens were covered in crud and severely underweight; three had eye infections so severe their eyes had ruptured; and two of the kittens were so sick they were hardly able to move. We promptly thanked the lady for helping the kittens and then tried to figure out what to do next.

Fortunately, Dr. Amy Holstein, a local veterinarian, had recently started volunteering with us. As she had vast experience as an emergency and small animal vet, we thought this would be right up her alley. We called her to explain our predicament. She was available and could come over right away.

After one look at the little kittens, she said these were some of the worst eyes she had ever seen. While we were all completely grossed out by what we saw, Amy just said, "But, it's not as bad as it looks; most of the damage has already been done." The task ahead of us was to clean out the eyes, ears, and noses so we could really see the extent of their illnesses.

We lined up every surgical wipe, bandage, and medication we had and went to work. We set up an assembly line to process the kittens. Bob gave the kittens a flea bath and scrubbed the snot off them at the same time. I cleaned ears and "lifted the tail" to see if we had a boy or a girl. Amy was at the end of the line figuring out what was wrong with each kitten, coming up with a treatment protocol, and in some cases, stuffing the remains of their eyes back in place.

In the end we had: three cases of double pneumonia, one had a severe hip deformity, two were completely blind, all seven had varying degrees of eye damage, and, oh yeah, they also had almost every parasite known to cats.

The next few days were critical for the kittens. Soon they knew the routine of daily antibiotics, eye flushes and force feedings. As their health improved, their antics became more entertaining. Before long it took two people to care for the kittens. One person would open the cage door and block their escape, while the other would extract the kittens from the other person's hair and give them their medication.

They soon outgrew their cages and were moved to our quarantine room to give them more space to run and play. In deference to their race track origins they were named after famous race horses: Seattle Slew, Secretariat, Seabiscuit, Spectacular Bid, Ruffian, Native Dancer and Queen Doreen.

Now that the kittens were over their illnesses and ready to enjoy life, their room soon became the most popular one at the sanctuary. After all, these kittens did things the adult cats wouldn't be caught dead doing. They really seemed to have a thing for hair. Several volunteers with long tresses came out of the room with completely different hairstyles. Seattle Slew even managed to get stuck in one of the volunteer's hair. For awhile we thought we'd need a pair of scissors to free him. The kittens were well on their way to a full recovery. They were spayed and neutered without complications. Now we just had to deal with the eye problems.

While we were trying to figure out how Rude Ranch was going to afford the vet care for seven pairs of very damaged kitten eyes, we got a lucky break: Dr. Anne Weigt, one of the best veterinary ophthalmologists in the area, agreed to look at them, really cheaply. She was coerced into this by Jill, who worked with her at the clinic, and Sue Ann, who sang with her in the church choir. It never hurt to have inside connections.

Dr. Weigt was going to work our kids in between her other cases. She would examine them and let us know if there was anything she could do for their eyes. The trip to the clinic went well; we were able to get the kittens rounded up and packed into a couple of large carriers. They arrived at the clinic ready to party. At some point the kittens caused a "ruckus." We don't know what really happened and no one at the clinic would give us the details. We just know that when we came to pick them up, the receptionist just looked at us and said "those kittens." All the vet techs just stared at us. Not the "have you lost your mind for starting an animal sanctuary" stare (we got that one a lot). This was the "these people have unleashed energy forces of unknown proportions upon us" stares. I guess we should have sent the kittens with a warning label, especially the one about their propensity for hair.

At least Dr. Weigt was nice enough to let us know what could be done for the kittens. Two of them needed to have the remaining eye tissue removed. The rest would be fine with varying degrees of blindness. Dr. Weigt did the surgeries to remove the damaged eyes, and also did laser surgeries on the three kittens with the most eye damage to hopefully give them a little more sight.

All the kittens made it through their ordeal and five were adopted into homes that thought their special needs made them more endearing. One of the kittens, Seabiscuit, was adopted by one of the vet techs at the clinic. I guess she thought the antics during their day at the clinic were cute.

One of the other kittens, Seattle Slew, was returned several months later for being too rambunctious. He soon found another home with a couple who thought his pouncing on feet in the middle of the night and climbing their Christmas tree was a blast. Soon we were getting almost weekly updates on his antics. He still stops by for our Photos with Santa event every year.

The two kittens with the most eye damage became permanent residents at Rude Ranch. Queenie and Secretariat had a number of serious health problems in addition to being blind. They both had severe heart ailments that could not be fixed. The kitty cardiologist didn't give them much hope, but put them on an aggressive medical treatment to at least give them the best chance possible.

Queenie became Bob's special buddy and followed him through the house like a little puppy. They were inseparable. She even slept on his head every night. Everyone was amazed when she learned to climb the poles and get up on the ramps. Most people found it hard to believe she was blind until they noticed the missing eyes. It was remarkable how well she adapted to her handicap. She could even figure out which dog was lying in the middle of the floor. We could never figure out exactly how she did it, but she would leap over the dog based on its size. Queenie was truly one of a kind.

Around the same time we were working with the race track kittens, three other kittens arrived: Larry, Moe and Curley. These three didn't have any lasting special needs, but did have some problems. All three arrived with a weird virus that made their tongues swell. At first it was cute to see all three kittens with their tongues hanging out, but their tongues kept swelling until they couldn't eat or drink. This was especially distressing to Curley who seemed very attached to his food.

Using our usual techniques, we fed the three kittens by syringe several times a day. Eventually the swelling went down enough for them to move their tongues and start eating a little. Curley, being the most upset about the whole not eating thing, couldn't contain himself when he first realized his mouth worked again. He chomped down and bit through my fingernail while I was giving him his medicine. I guess he thought he was ready for a higher protein diet.

Larry and Moe recovered without any lasting psychological affects from their illness. Curley, however, did have some lasting "issues." He could never get enough food, and the food was never served fast enough. While waiting for the food, he would cry like he hadn't eaten in days. He would stick his head under a can of food while we were dumping it out. This last move often resulted in half of the food landing on his head, leaving him with a spikey hairdo. He even trapped himself inside a flip-top trash can several times. He would push into the trash can to get the empty cans of cat food and then couldn't figure out how to get back out. Volunteers would lift the lid off the trash can to find Curley sound asleep on top of the trash.

Curley was soon known for his "drive by" food snatchings. His victims were human, feline and canine. As long as food was involved they were fair game. He stole food off other cats' plates while they were eating. If a volunteer was eating lunch at the kitchen table, he would snatch their food while it was enroute to their mouth. When the dogs were fed, he would settle down for a nosh off the dogs' plates while they looked on helplessly.

One day Curley met his biggest challenge, a whole chicken. One of our volunteers occasionally brought a roasted chicken as a treat for the cats. She would pick the meat off the chicken and go from room to room and give everyone a few pieces. One night, as she went to get a few paper plates for the chicken, Curley went to work. He had just eaten his usual huge supper and should have been full. But Curley couldn't resist the chicken. He ate, and ate and ate. By the time we caught him, half the chicken was gone. Curley wanted more, but he had finally hit his limit. His sides were bulging out like grapefruits. He was so full he didn't even want to jump off the table when we scolded him. (Most people who have ever eaten at a buffet can relate to his discomfort. It was one of those "I can't believe I ate the whole thing" moments.)

He spent the rest of the night curled up on the table looking miserable. We thought that would have cured Curley of his eating disorder, but the next day he was right back to stealing food from the volunteers.

Curley was adopted, food issues and all, by Jill, one of our volunteers, and to this day, still has issues with the speed at which his food is delivered to him.

Soon after Curley left, Stormy arrived on the scene. Susan, one of our foster moms and the sanctuary's attorney, agreed to care for this sweet, albeit rather large cat who was about to give birth. All went well for the first few days. Then Stormy started to show all the signs of giving birth: she didn't want to eat, she was restless and the biggest sign, kittens started popping out. Susan called to let us know that Stormy had given birth to four beautiful, healthy looking kittens.

Stormy's Nine Kittens
Photo Courtesy of Megan Roback

A few hours later Susan called to tell us Stormy had given birth to six beautiful, healthy kittens. Then Susan called to let us know Stormy was up to seven kittens. She just couldn't stop having kittens. I made arrangements to meet Susan to give her some baby bottles and kitten formula. Stormy was going to need some help raising seven kids.

By the time all was said and done, Stormy had given birth to nine beautiful, healthy kittens. We weren't sure, but that may be some sort of record.

Scruffy and the
Abandoned Car

After a summer of special needs kittens, it was time to begin planning our fall fundraising campaigns. This was the time of year when we usually filled our coffers for the next year. Fundraising was far tougher than we ever imagined. Sometimes it seemed the harder we tried, the less we accomplished. We were always looking for better ways to get the most bang for our buck.

We already had Photos with Santa down pat and even moved to doing our own digital version. Now we needed to come up with something to make Rude Ranch stand out at our events with the federal government. There were more than 4,000 charities participating in the Combined Federal Campaign and we needed to find our special angle.

We were small and had a minimal budget for give-away items to draw people over to us at the events. The larger groups had budgets for give-away items that were bigger than our entire yearly budget. How could we compete with that? Then we found our ace in the hole. Boomer, our Miniature Pinscher, was a huge suck up. He was cute, had a fabulous wardrobe (thanks to the many sweaters our volunteers and others had given him) and he was small enough we could easily carry him in and out of the buildings.

Before long we were known as the warm fuzzy group with the cute dog. Boomer eventually traveled to numerous agencies including the Pentagon, the IRS (where he met with the director), Navy Intelligence (a Rear Admiral took him for a walk), the CIA, the Secret Service, the FBI (he dressed as a bug), the EPA, and the NSA (he had a little trouble getting through security until General Hayden, the Director of NSA, escorted him into the building). He was so popular other charities even invited him to their events. Bob and I were only invited as an afterthought, mostly because Boomer hadn't mastered driving yet. Everything worked out great: Boomer worked cheaply; he would split a McDonald's burger with his driver on the way home. He was earning his "keep" and paying the cats back for all the toy mice he destroyed over the years. He was also instrumental in getting Rude Ranch some much needed publicity. Who could resist or forget Boomer?

Bob and I made it through the CFC campaign and the holidays without too many problems. We even breezed through January, the month of administrative nightmares: closing out the books, preparing for audits, filling out the dreaded IRS forms, sending out tax receipts, and applying to the CFC and state payroll campaigns for the next year. Picture mounds of paperwork sorted and rearranged by several four-legged office assistants and me banging my head on the desk. You get the picture.

Now I had to get all the paperwork in the mail and delivered before the dreaded deadlines. As I was returning from yet another trip to the post office, I noticed an old beat up car on the side of the road about two miles from Rude Ranch. That wasn't unusual; after all, we were in the country where people occasionally dumped trash and vehicles rather than pay to dispose of them. What was unusual was the pathetic looking dog lying next to the car. Was he abandoned with the car? Thinking we should do something, I continued home and told Bob about the dog (Bob was off to rescue the dog almost before I got the words out of my mouth).

In the meantime, I called the police to meet Bob at the car. We watched a lot of TV crime shows and we knew there was a 93% chance that whoever abandoned the car also could have left a dead body in the trunk. Upon arrival, the police agreed the car looked abandoned (the lack of license plates were a good clue). They would have the car towed and attempt to track down the owner. There was one problem: The dog was still guarding the car and wouldn't let the officers near it. They didn't want to shoot the dog, but they did have to complete their investigation. Could Bob help?

Bob went to work on the dog. Every time he got close, the dog started growling and snapping. Bob could tell the little Benji looking dog was just scared. It was time for Bob to pull out his secret weapon: Pupperonis. Before long the little dog was rolling over for tummy rubs and jumping in Bob's lap. The rolling around also led to his name. When he rolled on the ground, every twig, leaf, pebble, you name it, stuck in his fur. By the time he got up to run to the car, he looked a little scruffy. So Scruffy it was.

We later found out the car was registered to someone whose address was a suspected Meth lab. Nobody even wanted to check to see if Scruffy was their dog; so, Rude Ranch was granted custody of the little guy to find him a new home.

Rude Ranch's three established dogs didn't think much of the newcomer at first. After all, they had all the bases covered: Boomer was the star, Bruno was the gentle giant and Ceasar was the brainy kitten caretaker. Scruffy wasn't sure where he fit in either. He wasn't athletic enough to keep up with the bigger dogs, but he was too big for Boomer. He didn't impress anyone with his intelligence either. Ceasar was always tricking him into doing things just to get him in trouble. It seemed Scruffy's main talent was barking at everything. We finally put him up for adoption as a living door bell. He found a home and was quickly returned for barking too much. Maybe we should have seen that one coming.

Once back, he barked even more. Most potential adopters that came to see him would listen to his barking and say no thanks. One of Scuffy's other talents was helping people find Bob. Wherever Bob went, Scruffy was there. If we wanted to find Bob, we'd just look for Scruffy and we knew Bob was on the other side of the door. When we took all of this into consideration, Bob and I adopted our fourth dog.

Scruffy Just After He Arrived

At some point Scruffy figured out that Ceasar was the favorite dog of most of our volunteers. As such, Ceasar got special treats and privileges. Scruffy decided it would be in his best interests to stick to Ceasar and ride his wagon. Ceasar wasn't thrilled with that idea, but eventually grew to love the little guy.

After the excitement with Scruffy died down, we hit another hurdle, or actually a rod. The trusty four wheel drive Suburban, the vehicle that brought many animals to the safety of Rude Ranch, hauled thousands of pounds of kitty food and litter, pulled stranded cars out of snow banks and forged a river, threw a rod through the engine. We didn't understand completely what that meant, but knew it wasn't good. For a sanctuary whose other vehicle was a two-seater sports car, this was a show stopper. We needed another big vehicle and we needed it soon.

We started cruising internet sites and classified ads for a vehicle. One morning we hit pay dirt. A ten cylinder, low mileage, fifteen passenger van with a towing capacity of 10,000 pounds was for sale. I didn't know what all that meant, but it sounded big. It belonged to a church group, but it was so big that no one wanted to drive it. It had a couple of stains on the carpet, could we deal with that? (We're an animal sanctuary. A couple of stains were nothing.) Bob bought the van on the spot. Shortly after buying the van we started training our volunteers on the finer points of piloting an aircraft carrier.

Hurricane Katrina – The Adventure Begins

Bob and I had just returned from a quick vacation to Niagara Falls in August of 2005, when we got word of a massive storm developing in the Caribbean. Although we weren't in the direct path of the storm, we went ahead and prepared anyway. A few days later we started to hear of the absolute devastation for people and animals in New Orleans and the Gulf Coast region. Hurricane Katrina had hit the Gulf Coast, and hit it hard. Soon a call went out to animal groups for help.

Although Rude Ranch was a very small organization, we felt the need to do something to help out the animals. Shortly after news of the devastation reached us, we started working on a game plan. We had just bought a huge van that could haul a lot of supplies. We also had access to much needed medical supplies through our vets, which were not readily available to the general public. We had some experience in disaster situations and the ability to provide critical care for animals. Bob and another volunteer (also named Bob) would head down to the Hurricane area, deliver supplies, and help with whatever was needed. Before the "Bobs" could hit the road, they had to get ready.

Our first order of business was to increase the amount of stuff (supplies and/or animals) the Bobs could haul at one time.

Volunteer Debbie and her husband Dennis had a twenty-eight foot box trailer they could loan us. Our main problem was to get the braking system on the trailer to talk to the electrical system on the van. This required something called a brake controller. I wasn't sure what it was, but it did have nice flashing lights. There were also things called stabilizers. They were supposed to make the trailer easier to handle on the open road. I wasn't sure exactly how they worked, but I don't think they were supposed to fall off every time we went around a corner. They just needed some "minor" adjustments before the trip.

Once we had the van and the trailer working together, it was time to get the inside of the trailer ready. This trailer was used to haul sprint cars, not necessarily an easy retrofit for animals. We devised a game plan to temporarily convert the trailer into an animal transport vehicle. Volunteers Stephanie and Pam joined in and started installing dog crates and carriers along the sides of the trailer (bungee cords and zip ties were wonderful inventions). Whether Debbie and Dennis realized it or not, the tracks they installed to secure the sprint cars were perfectly aligned to accommodate large dog crates. It was an exact fit. Once all the crates were secured in the trailer, we were ready to start loading supplies.

We notified many of the local animal groups about our plan to help the animals devastated by Hurricane Katrina. They all pitched in and started delivering supplies for Rude Ranch to take with us. In addition to the medical supplies, we were getting tons of donated food and blankets to take along, meaning we had a lot of people coming and going. Ceasar was in his glory playing the traffic controller and directing people where to put the stuff. His only real problem occurred when volunteer Lisa stopped by to drop off some supplies. She was driving her trailer loaded with two horses. Ceasar was totally freaked out by the horses. We weren't sure if he'd had a bad experience at some point in his life or had never met a horse before. We were all impressed with the speed he reached backtracking up the driveway. It would have been even faster if he hadn't run over Scruffy along the way.

During the preparations for the trip, it became obvious we were in for some major communication problems: There were two Bobs. That could get confusing. Who did what? Oh, it was Bob, which really cleared things up. I made the decision to develop creative code names for our two Bobs. My Bob would be code named Rude Dude Bob; the other Bob would simply be known as Bob, or the "other" Bob.

Eventually all the supplies were loaded, their destination determined (LSU Vet School) and directions were locked and loaded into Bob's GPS system (the other Bob, not Rude Dude Bob. See what I mean about the confusion). The van and trailer were talking to each other, the Bobs loaded their stuff, Ceasar finished directing traffic, and we were ready to send them on their way. It was almost anti-climatic to watch their "rig" pull out of the driveway and disappear down the road.

They made pretty good time for the first hour, and then they hit the "great wall" of traffic always present around Washington D.C. They started to wonder if they would even make it out of Virginia that night. They finally made it out of the traffic jam and headed through the mountains of western Virginia and into Tennessee.

Things were going well until Rude Dude Bob noticed the gas gauge was dropping way too fast. They made an important discovery; when you're pulling a fully loaded trailer, your mileage dropped from 15 MPG to about 5 MPG. Now they had to rethink their gas emergency plan. They had extra cans of gas in the trailer just in case there was a shortage of it where they were heading. It seemed like a reasonable idea at the time. They just hadn't anticipated the affect of the loaded trailer on their mileage. A stop to pick up some extra gas cans at a local Wal-Mart was in their future.

They were back to making good time until they neared Birmingham, Alabama; that's when they learned a little more about pulling a large trailer:

Lesson no.1: Check the tires closely if the trailer hasn't been used for a long time. It was no fun to blow a tire when pulling a 15,000 pound trailer. It had the distinct effect of raising the blood pressure a little bit.

Lesson no. 2: The trailer jack won't lift a fully loaded trailer. Fortunately, someone had conveniently left a block of wood on the side of the road that worked great to supplement the jack. A little ingenuity can sometimes cover for a lack of planning.

Lesson no. 3: It can be difficult to find parking when you are pulling a really big trailer attached to a really big van. Gas stations can be a little difficult to maneuver through too.

The good news; the other Bob and his wife Sue Ann had lived in Birmingham for several years. He thought he remembered a National Tire and Battery a few miles up the road. A quick stop and the Bobs had a brand new tire and still had the spare for a backup.

They were cruising through southern Alabama when they received a call from the Hurricane rescue coordinators. The Bobs hadn't even reached their destination and they were being reassigned. They were needed to transport animals between various rescue and staging areas. Could they re-route from the LSU Vet School to Tylertown, Mississippi?

They were given directions to the St. Francis Animal Sanctuary in Tylertown where the Best Friends Animal Sanctuary was setting up a rescue center. Fortunately, the Bobs had the GPS system with them, so they plotted a new route faster then Mr. Sulu on the Enterprise and they were on their way.

The next morning they pulled into Tylertown bright and early. The scene there could best be described as organized chaos. The search and rescue (SAR) team was attempting to get out of the camp, but kept running into people (morons) like the Bobs showing up and blocking their way. It took a few deft maneuvers, but the Bobs and the SAR team finally navigated around each other.

The Bobs located the supply area, backed in the trailer, and began the fun process of unloading five tons of cargo in the 100 plus degree heat. Then they wandered around the camp looking for their contact to get their assignments. They found him looking a little frazzled with all the hustle and bustle around the camp. That was when they found out everything had changed yet again in the twelve hours since they spoke on the phone. The Bobs were no longer needed to transport the animals, that plan had changed due to some political issues.

The Bobs were wondering if they should head out for the LSU Vet School as originally planned or if there was something they could do at the base camp in Tylertown. That was when they met Kitt. She was in charge of the base camp and was responsible for coordinating the care of the 400 plus animals already in the camp. She also had to plan for the seventy plus new animals being rescued each day. I guess that answered the Bobs' question; they would be staying in Tylertown.

Kitt took one look at the Rude Dude Bob and asked if he had any experience handling aggressive dogs. Bob admitted he wasn't officially a dog handler, but had spent a lot of time wrestling with dogs that didn't want to pose with Santa. Who knew doing a stint as Santa would actually look good on a resume?

He was sent to Sherry, the dog rescue coordinator, to get a crash course on his duties for the area that became known as "Pit Bull Row." Yes, you guessed it; the area consisted of a lot of Pit Bulls and many of the dog breeds considered dangerous or potentially aggressive. They also had one little Yorkie in the area that looked pathetic stuck in a run between two Pit Bulls. He earned his private run on Pit Bull Row by biting everyone he met, including Sherry, twice. At least he had his own area with plenty of room to run. This was also one of those small world encounters; Bob and Sherry had met years earlier when we vacationed at Best Friends in Utah.

The "Vicious" Little Yorkie

The other Bob pulled various duties with the cats that included helping care for them, constructing awnings to give them shade and taking pictures of them to help families locate their pets. Helping families reunite with their pets was one of the toughest tasks after Hurricane Katrina. It was like trying to find a needle in a hay stack. There were thousands of animals wandering the area, most with no ID and very little to distinguish them from each other. Still, taking pictures of the animals greatly increased the chance that families would be reunited with their pets.

Every day was busy and incredibly hot. The heat index would climb to 115 degrees or more during the day. The Gatorade disappeared by the pallet load. A lot of people and animals were having problems with heat stroke. There just wasn't any way to cool off. Then one day some volunteers from Texas arrived with a trailer full of kiddy pools. The volunteers quickly filled them up and the dogs finally had a break from the heat. Rude Dude Bob didn't mention it, but I have a feeling some of the volunteers joined the dogs.

Rude Dude Bob was busy caring for the dogs in the morning and building new dog runs in the afternoon. He had barely taken time to visit the cats. Then while eating supper one night, he overheard several of the cat caretakers talking about a cat that was severely ill and might not make it through the night. The cat was in kidney failure, had double pneumonia, animal bites all over her body, could barely breathe and wouldn't eat. She was semi-feral and had already bitten several people who were trying to help her. Hearing her story, Bob immediately felt sorry for her and offered his experience if they thought he could help.

Adelle and Linda, two of the cat caretakers, graciously allowed Bob to finish eating and then whisked him off to meet the cat. That was where Bob first met Dr. Ron Lott ("Dr. Ron"), the vet taking care of the camp's feline population. He didn't have much hope for the little cat, but if Bob wanted to give it a try more power to him.

Bob settled down with the cat securely wrapped in a towel, gave her some fluids and went to work trying to get some food into her. She immediately responded by peeing all over him (hey, it was better than the bites she was giving everybody else). He managed to get a little bit of food to actually make it down her throat and into her stomach; the rest was evenly divided between the cat, the floor and Bob's shirt.

Throughout the next twenty-four hours Bob and the cat, who had been dubbed Dame Katrina, went through the same routine every few hours. By the next morning, Katrina seemed a little brighter, or at least she seemed to bite her caretakers a little harder. Surprisingly, the caretakers didn't seem to mind; they took it as a sign she was on the road to recovery.

For the rest of their stay in Tylertown, Bob and Katrina worked out an agreement: he would give her fluids and force some food into her mouth, and she would refrain from biting and peeing on him. Although she wasn't out of the woods yet, each day she seemed a little stronger.

One constant in Tylertown was that more animals arrived every day. Two of the people working on the search and rescue team were Don and Mike. Don arrived with Dr. Ron and had put his trapping skills to use on the search and rescue team. Mike was a relatively new employee with Best Friends and was sent to Tylertown to take care of the cats. Shortly after arriving, he was reassigned to help with the difficult task of rescuing the animals that desperately needed help. The search and rescue teams were focusing on the areas completely devastated and under as much as ten feet of water. The animals in these areas were in the greatest need with no source of food or fresh water.

Every day they headed out in the morning and returned around 2:00 a.m. with the day's "catch." Bob noticed that most nights they were bringing in a lot of dogs, but not all that many cats. He jokingly asked them if the cats were too smart for them or just harder to catch. The next day they came back with twenty-seven cats. Mike said Don must have taken Bob's joke as a personal challenge and was determined to help the less than appreciative cats. The cats, in general, were much tougher to rescue than the average dog. Some of the dogs would put up a fight, but just as many would happily run up to the rescuers for whatever treats they were offering (or sometimes just for a pat on the head and a hug). The cats would run and hide, or if you were lucky enough to grab one, they would bite, scratch and do anything to escape. They just didn't realize the people were there to help them.

The time had flown by and it was time for the Bobs to leave. Although Dame Katrina was doing better, Dr. Ron felt she still needed more care than was available at the staging area. It was decided it would be best for Katrina if she returned to Rude Ranch with the Bobs.

That wasn't exactly a problem for Rude Dude Bob. After all the time he spent keeping Katrina alive, they would have had to tie him up to keep him and Katrina apart.

Of course things couldn't be that simple; the prevailing politics stated that no animals could leave the staging area except by special medical waiver, signed by a FEMA vet. No one could find a FEMA vet. Just in case a FEMA vet couldn't be found, a top secret plan was hatched by most of the camp to smuggle Katrina out to the Bobs while they slowly drove by the cat building. Fortunately, Laura, one of the dog groomers from Chicago, was able track down Dr. Pema, a FEMA vet who quickly approved Katrina's medical waiver. The covert plan was scrapped and a very sick Dame Katrina was escorted to the van by Kitt, Dr. Ron, and several of the caretakers. She had become a symbol of survival for the camp and was a very popular little girl. Everyone said their good-byes and the Bobs hit the road.

A Very Sick Katrina after a Meal with Bob
Photo courtesy of Clay Myers

The Bobs started the long trip back to Maryland transporting one cat in their specially equipped van and trailer combination that could haul up to 140 animals. They were willing to take more, but as I stated before, the politics were still a major issue in the area.

The Bobs made good time on the return trip until they blew out another tire. It wasn't all that far from the spot where the tire blew out on the way to New Orleans. At least they knew where to find a repair shop.

The Bobs and Katrina survived the rest of the 1,100 mile journey back to Maryland. Katrina's health continued to improve, although she could still scare the crap out of most people. We took her to see Dr. Harrison and he confirmed most of what Dr. Ron had diagnosed in Tylertown. Katrina had double pneumonia, a severe sinus infection, was severely malnourished and in complete kidney failure. We were still waiting for some good news. Oh yeah, she was still alive. Despite all her problems, Katrina steadily improved and slowly started eating on her own. That, you see, was a big victory for me too, since I was designated the official Katrina feeder once the Bobs returned from New Orleans.

Hurricane Katrina – The Adventure Continues

B ob did a few of our Combined Federal Campaign events and even did a couple of special request engagements with the IRS and FEMA. They were interested in what was happening on the animal rescue front in New Orleans. Bob did the speaking engagements even though he wasn't a fan of speaking in public. He took Boomer along for moral support.

Around the middle of September, we received another call from the disaster coordinators: many of the initial first responders to the Katrina disaster were starting to leave (something about wanting to get back to their lives and jobs), but people were still needed to rescue and care for the animals being pulled from the flood waters. Would Bob be willing to come back? Could he bring anyone else?

Although it was the middle of the Combined Federal Campaign fundraising season, Bob could go back for a total of ten days before things really started to get busy here. We knew a couple of people from the Anne Arundel County SPCA, Annette and Lyra, who wanted to go, and a couple of people we worked with at the Census Bureau, Greg and Jan, who were also thinking about heading south.

The five of them worked out a game plan for their "vacation" to New Orleans. Greg and Jan left first. They were ready to go and anxious to help with the animals. Annette and Lyra left a few days later around

4:30 in the morning. Bob had a few things to finish up that morning and didn't hit the road until about 7:00 a.m. They didn't have specific travel plans; they just knew at some point they would all meet up in Tylertown.

Bob figured he would catch up with Annette and Lyra somewhere along the way. He spent most of the day in hot pursuit of the SPCA van. It seemed as though he would never catch them, but he finally caught sight of their van just south of Chattanooga, Tennessee.

They spent the night in Tuscaloosa, Alabama and got an early start in the morning. They pulled into the Tylertown staging area a few hours later. Just after they arrived, Bob ran into Kitt. She was still running the camp and needed someone to run the cat area. She thought that would be right up Bob's alley. Bob agreed. He didn't have anything against the dogs, but the cat area was inside a building. No air conditioning, but no sun beating down on him either. Annette and Lyra hooked up with Mike, the guy doing the search and rescue on Bob's first trip, and helped him in the dog area. Then Bob ran into Greg and Jan. They had made it to Tylertown and were busy helping out with the dogs.

The day flew by and it was time to settle in for the night. Bob wandered back to do the final check on the cats and then crashed in his bedroom, the back of the Rude Ranch van. Bob said it was fairly comfortable with the air mattress and a few other adjustments he made for the trip. I wasn't buying into it; I was afraid he would suggest the van for our next vacation.

The next day Bob ran into some people he worked with on his first trip to Tylertown. Beth was still busy working in the office area tracking down families and reuniting people with their pets. Cathy and Mary were working in the office keeping track of all the animals brought into the rescue center. Many of the animals were now being released to rescue groups all over the country (even some in Canada) and had to be tracked closely to make sure their families had a chance to find them. Cathy was also sent to Tylertown as Best Friends' on-site reporter. She was to write about the rescues and keep people updated through the various blogs on their web-site. As the on-site reporter she had to have an assistant, a little Chihuahua named Lois Lane, who was one of the first dogs rescued after the Hurricane.

Then Bob ran into Clay, the Best Friends staff photographer. He provided us with some great pictures from Bob's first trip to Tylertown

(Bob would always forget to take pictures when he did the disaster response thing). Best Friends sent Clay to photographically record all the activities related to the rescues after Hurricane Katrina. Unfortunately for him, he let it slip that he also had experience with construction and plumbing. He was recruited to build much needed showers for the volunteers at the camp. You could only go so long with over 100 people and one available shower stall. After all, it was over 100 degrees most days.

It had been more than three weeks since the Hurricane hit and by now many of the rescued cats and dogs had been in the muck and gunk for the entire time. They had inhaled all kinds of mold, were severely malnourished and were generally freaked out. Most of the cats Bob cared for were no exception. Most had various medical needs and some required medications, fluids, and force feeding around the clock. Bob usually took the midnight shift himself. One night as he was walking back to his bedroom (van), he heard a lot of yelling and commotion; it sounded like someone yelling "catch the pig."

Bob realized what was happening when a 300 plus pound Pot Bellied pig ran into him at full speed. In an effort to slow the pig down, Bob sat on her (at least they were pretty evenly matched in weight class). While riding a pig wasn't in the same league as a bucking bronco, apparently they were somewhat difficult to hang on to. It took twenty people almost thirty minutes, before "Suzie the pig" was finally herded back to her pen. Bob had jokingly earned the title "The Pig Whisperer."

Jeff and Ethan, two of the Best Friends employees, had been doing most of the search and rescue work since the Hurricane struck. They went in almost every day and usually handled the tougher cases. Several times they were featured on CNN, *Animal Planet* and various other media venues that had become very interested in how the animal rescue efforts were progressing in the New Orleans area.

One of the animals they rescued was a very shy and very freaked out Cattle Dog. Jeff and Ethan spent close to two hours trying to catch her. Every time they had her cornered, she would jump fences or shoot past them. They finally had her when she ran into a house and went up the stairs into an attic crawl space. It took a little more work with a catch pole (a tool used to secure dogs that weren't all that cooperative) and a lot of wrestling and grunting, but they finally had her. It was another reluctant, but successful rescue.

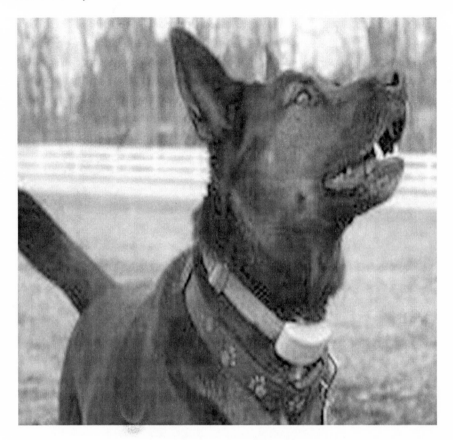

Sweetie Hanging out at Rude Ranch

The next day Kitt moved this incredibly freaked out young Cattle Dog into a crate outside the cat area. She felt the dog was too terrified to stay in a full-sized run, and was hoping she would adapt to the commotion of the camp quicker in the crate.

Bob met her first thing in the morning. After all, she was right outside of the cat area where he was spending about eighteen hours a day. He would stop by her crate every chance he had and even started sharing his snacks with her during his breaks.

On the fifth day, Bob went to share a sandwich with her and was surprised that her crate was gone. Not knowing what happened, he went looking for her. Fortunately, he didn't have to look far; as soon as she heard his voice, the dog vaulted over the wall of her new kennel and launched herself at him, almost giving Bob a concussion. That was when I got a call from Bob asking how I felt about his bringing a Cattle

Dog back with him. What could I say? I told him it was up to him (that way I could always say I never really gave him my approval). He started calling her Sweetie and the name stuck.

Then one night a very sick little cat was brought in from New Orleans. Dr. Candice Armstrong ("Dr. Candice"), a vet from the Atlanta area, was handling the medical needs of the cats at the rescue center now. When she first took the cat out of the carrier, they weren't all that sure she was still alive. Dr. Candice did a quick check with her stethoscope and determined that yes; the cat's heart was still beating. Now things started moving at the speed of light. This poor little cat was in really bad shape and needed a lot of help and the faster the better. Dr. Candice inserted a catheter into one of the cat's veins and started immediate fluid therapy. They put her in a warm, quiet cage and began around the clock critical care. They thought she looked like a Charlotte.

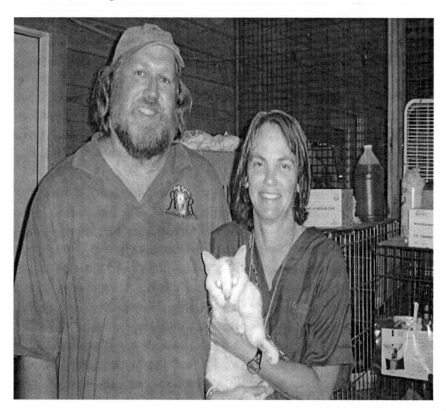

Bob with Dr. Candace and Charlotte in Tylertown

Four more cats arrived that night that weren't in much better shape than Charlotte.

One was Old Boy, a cat that appeared to be older than dirt. He was covered in gunk and was drooling uncontrollably. He had probably been in severely contaminated water so they began treating him for poisoning and gave him a lot of baths to get the caustic gunk off his skin.

The second cat was Orange Boy (I guess you can kind of see a trend in the naming convention. They had a lot of cats coming into the camp and had to pick names that were easily remembered). He was as skinny as a rail and looked like he hadn't eaten since Hurricane Katrina passed through the area. They started him on fluid therapy and frequent small meals to help put some weight back on him. Betsy, a volunteer from the Boston area, immediately fell for this little guy and offered to personally take over his care. This was one of those risks of doing rescue work, falling in love with your patients.

The third critical care cat was Bite Boy. As you might guess from his name he arrived with multiple bite wounds all over his body. It looked worse than it was, but they did have to shave him and stitch up the worst of the wounds. He was a little on the aggressive side, and wasn't all that cooperative with his treatment. At least they were able to treat his wounds and give him his medications without losing too much blood themselves (maybe they named him Bite Boy for another reason).

Psycho was the fourth cat. She earned her name for a variety of reasons, but I believe Bob picked her name during her bath(s). You see, this cat came in completely saturated with gunk and was as black as soot from a chimney. It was getting late and everyone was more than a little tired. Bob told everyone to crash and he would give the cat her bath. It took about four soakings and a pint of Bob's blood, but he finally had this beautiful, mostly white, long-haired cat to put back in the cage. Then Bob crashed and took a much needed nap.

When Bob arrived in the cat room the next morning there was a slight feeling of panic. They couldn't find the black cat that arrived the night before. There was this pretty white cat in the cage. Where did the black cat go? Nobody would believe Bob when he told them the story. There was no way that could be the same cat. They finally accepted Bob's story. I don't know if they ever really believed him, but I guess they couldn't come up with any other explanation.

The next day there was more than the normal commotion in the camp. Everyone was busy preparing for the arrival of two of Best Friends' co-founders, Francis and Silva Battista. For those of you not familiar with Best Friends, its founders were to the animal rescue community what Bill Gates is to the computer industry. They were highly respected for their efforts to help animals and a lot of us animal rescue people were just a little jealous of all their resources. The atmosphere in the camp was a little like that of celebrities passing through a small town.

The Battistas were there to evaluate how things were going at the rescue center and determine what additional resources were needed to improve the animal rescue efforts. As part of their evaluation, Sherry brought Francis over to the cat area and asked Bob to give him a tour. Bob didn't know what to expect. He was pleasantly surprised to find that Francis was a real cat person and seemed genuinely interested in Bob's ideas for improving the cat care at the camp.

At this point, one of Bob's primary concerns was to find a person who could oversee the cat area when he left. Francis said he would look into that as well as the other ideas Bob and he discussed.

Then one day as Bob was getting ready to start his morning routine, Sherry asked if he would help out with a Staffordshire Terrier that needed to be walked. This dog was a little on the crazy side and didn't like people coming at him in his crate. Sherry coaxed "Spuds" out of his crate and Bob took him for a walk. It was nothing exciting, just a normal out with the dog type of walk.

After Bob returned with Spuds, Sherry gave him a rawhide bone as a little treat for being a good boy (Spuds, not Bob). That was when things got interesting. Somehow the dog managed to get the bone stuck vertically between his upper and lower jaw. The dog was obviously in some distress, but not really freaking out yet. Bob and Sherry just looked at each other. Who wanted to stick their hand in a dog's mouth that had the bone-crushing strength of an alligator? Bob decided to "volunteer" for this duty while Sherry held the dog's leash. Fortunately, all went smoothly and Spuds was back to being a happy dog. Just to make sure, Bob had Sherry count his fingers; yep, all ten were still where they should be.

Bob knew he would need to head back to Maryland soon (after all, I did need him to escort Boomer to all the charity events). As part of the preparations for his departure, he headed to the airport in Jackson, Mississippi to pick up Elaine, who was driving in from Arizona. She was the friend of Barbara, a Rude Ranch volunteer. When Barbara told her Bob would be driving back from Mississippi by himself with a bunch of animals, she said she would be happy to help on the return trip. She was planning a trip to Maryland anyway and would rent a car and meet Bob at the closest airport.

Bob also realized the 1,100 mile drive from Tylertown to Rude Ranch was a long way with a bunch of very sick animals. There probably weren't any hotels that would let him hang out with as many animals as he'd be bringing back with him. Then Bob had an idea (it does happen from time to time). Two people who had volunteered with Rude Ranch, Hope and Phil, now lived near Knoxville, Tennessee. That was pretty much the halfway point of his trip. He made a call: "Remember when you said if there was ever anything you could do for Rude Ranch, to give you a call? Well, would you have space for me, another person and maybe twenty to thirty really sick animals?" To Bob's surprise, they agreed; no questions or concerns other than when he would arrive. They had a heated RV garage that would work perfectly for the animals.

Now back to Bob's other dilemma: he still didn't have anyone to take over the cat area when he left. Just when Bob had started to give up hope, Francis showed up and said he had found someone to take over for him. Bob was ready to go meet this person and start filling them in on their new duties. Bob asked when he could meet his replacement and Francis just said, "We've already met." Francis was volunteering to take over the cat area until one of the Best Friends caretakers arrived from Utah.

Now it was time for Bob to leave the rescue center. There were still about 100 cats under his care with twenty of them still fairly sick. To ease the workload of the people taking over for him (and to minimize Bob's worrying about what happened to them), he offered to take the more critical care cats back to Rude Ranch with him.

As he was loading up the necessary food, fluids and medical supplies for the trip, he started thinking about the Cattle Dog and how lonely she was (and how attached Bob had become to her). Before long he started configuring the van to include one much larger dog crate to accommodate the Cattle Dog. After all, he had already sought my approval earlier in the week. Now it was up to him.

He asked Sherry about adding Sweetie to the list along with the twenty cats; it took her all of two seconds to approve the "adoption" and get started on the paperwork. Most of the animals Bob brought back were released under the Rude Ranch name. Sherry put Sweetie under Bob's name. She knew Sweetie was to become Bob's buddy rather than a dog we would put up for adoption (I guess Sherry had Bob figured out; wish she would give me some pointers).

Sherry and a Veterinarian from Avid, Microchippng a Rescued Dog
Photo Courtesy of Clay Meyers

Soon, Bob, Elaine, Sweetie, and the twenty cats were on their way back to Maryland. Their trip went pretty smoothly. They stopped at Phil and Hope's home in Tennessee and spent the night there. Hope even made Bob's favorite meal, macaroni and cheese. They left the next morning and arrived at Rude Ranch to more than twenty volunteers who had gathered to welcome them home and help unload our new kids.

Things were incredibly busy for the next four months. We had a new dog, twenty critical care animals and a full fundraising schedule for the fall season. Our in-take room was full and then some. We had twelve double cage setups so cats could have one room for a bathroom and the other for their bedroom/dining room. With all the cats Bob brought back from New Orleans, we had all those setups full and a bunch of dog crates stacked around the room for the rest of our new guests. Fortunately, most of the cats were recovering well and we had even found homes for some of them.

One of the cats that found a home was Bite Boy. This wasn't a normal adoption; it was a Hurricane Katrina reunion.

The Tyson family, from New Orleans, had been desperately trying to locate their cat Garfield since the Hurricane hit the Gulf Coast. When the order went out to evacuate, they loaded up their car, including their pets. The one exception was Garfield. He shot out a window and they couldn't catch him. They eventually had to give up the search and head out of town before the Hurricane struck.

They were now living with a friend in Front Royal, Virginia, but were still trying to find Garfield. The husband went back to their home to see what was left and to hopefully find their cat. He couldn't find Garfield at their home; so, he started checking at the local rescue centers. None of the cats were Garfield. Then one of the volunteers at the Tylertown rescue center started showing him pictures of cats that were sent to various rescues. He saw one he thought could be Garfield.

He called his wife to give her the information. He told her that a cat matching Garfield's description was at a place called Rude Ranch, about two hours away in Maryland. The wife called us and set up an appointment to visit Rude Ranch the next day.

You can imagine their disappointment when they looked at the cat and realized he wasn't their Garfield. Then the cat in the cage next door let out a big "MEOW." The Tyson's took a closer look at the cat. It didn't really look like their cat, but acted like him. This cat was skinny and had bite wounds all over his body. With all the injuries and weight loss, they just couldn't be sure. I got the cat out of the cage to give them a better look. Now, this was a cat that didn't want anything to do with most people, but with the Tyson's he rolled over like a kitten and begged them for tummy rubs. It was clear to me that even if they weren't positive he was their cat, Garfield, the cat we called Bite Boy, was.

The Tyson's took Garfield back to their temporary home in Front Royal, Virginia about ninety percent sure he was their cat. They still had a little bit of doubt because of his physical changes.

The next day they called us to confirm it was their Garfield. As soon as they brought the cat into their temporary home, their Rottweiler immediately went to Garfield and started grooming him. When they snuggled up together that night, the Tyson's were positive they had their Garfield back home.

The Tyson Family with Their Cat Garfield

Another Hurricane cat that found a home was Bob's buddy Psycho, the black cat that miraculously turned into a white cat overnight. Beth, a new volunteer at Rude Ranch, felt a connection with Psycho right away. It wasn't long before Beth decided it was time to adopt a cat from the place where she volunteered. Psycho went to her new home with one major change; she was now Coco, a much more appropriate name for a cute little girl.

Hurricane Katrina – The Adventure Ends

It was the middle of January, 2006 and time for Bob to make his third trek to New Orleans. This time, with a little twist, he had a feline passenger to keep him company. Minew, one of the Katrina kitties from his second trip, was heading back to her family. We had tracked her family down a couple of months ago. They described her perfectly and she was found about two blocks from their house. Bob made arrangements to meet Minew's dad near New Orleans where he was living with his wife and two other cats in one of those infamous FEMA trailers. Once Minew was reunited with her family, Bob would go on to Celebration Station, a new rescue center in Metairie, a suburb of New Orleans. This rescue center was a joint project between Best Friends and a new group, Animal Rescue New Orleans (ARNO). They originated from all the devastation and animal rescue needs after Hurricane Katrina.

Bob and Minew left early one morning with the hopes of beating the Washington D.C. rush hour traffic. This time he was successful and made good time all the way to Tuscaloosa, Alabama. Bob talked it over with Minew and they thought it would be a good place to spend the night (I tried not to comment, but Bob does talk to the animals a lot. I really hoped he didn't think they talked back to him). There was a LaQuinta Inn that allowed pets and they were only a few hours from where Bob would meet Minew's dad the next morning. All was going as planned.

They woke up early the next morning, anxious to get on the road to meet Minew's dad. They planned to meet at a local Home Depot. Bob pulled into the parking lot and waited in anticipation of this happy reunion. He even had his camera ready to take a picture (he wasn't going to miss the opportunity this time). The gentleman arrived, pulled up next to the van and hopped into the passenger seat ready to meet his old buddy Minew.

Then disaster struck for Minew and Bob. Although the cat looked identical to his buddy Minew, he just wasn't sure; it didn't seem like it was her. He called his wife to get more details on how she remembered Minew, and she confirmed his concerns. This wasn't their cat. He felt horrible that Bob made the 1,100 mile trip to reunite a family and it wasn't their cat. He'd love to take her anyway, but he was already living with two cats in a small trailer and still hoped to find his third cat Minew.

Minew Navigating from the Dash of the Rude Ranch Van

Bob left, determined to help them find the real Minew. He headed for their old neighborhood near the St. Bernard High School. Bob also had to resolve his new problem; what to do with his feline passenger while volunteering for the next eight days. But, the first priority was to check out the neighborhood and see what he could do about locating the real Minew.

Bob arrived in front of their house and noticed a few cats running around, but none matching Minew's description. Then a few people started heading towards Bob. They didn't appear all that friendly. Bob greeted them and got an ear full about rescue groups going around stealing animals and that he had better not be there to take their cats and dogs or he would be in for a load of trouble. Now Bob's a pretty laid back person and generally doesn't go out looking for trouble. He assured the people he was only there trying to help animals in need and to help reunite people with their pets. He explained the issue with Minew and even introduced them to the cat he was now calling the "faux (fake) Minew." They seemed to mellow out and even started telling Bob stories of their experiences during and after Hurricane Katrina.

It became obvious that he wasn't going to have any luck finding the real Minew. Nobody in the neighborhood had seen a cat by that description since the Hurricane. Hopefully, she ended up with a rescue group or with a kind soul who took pity on her.

It was time to head to Celebration Station and get his assignment for the next week. Bob only made it a few miles when a sheriff's car passed him and then cut him off. No sirens, no lights; just cut in front of him and blocked the road. Bob hit the brakes and everything in the back came shooting to the front. Fortunately, Minew was safely settled in the passenger seat and didn't seem to notice the abrupt stop.

Bob was starting to freak out a little, partly because of his experience with the slightly angry mob a little while ago. Was this something related to what another animal rescuer had done and Bob was going to get caught in the crossfire? He tried to calmly collect his thoughts while the sheriff exited his vehicle and approached him. He was surprised and relieved when the sheriff asked if Bob happened to have any cat food he could buy from him. The sheriff was feeding a colony of cats in his yard and was running out of food. The nearest pet store was a half-hour away.

Bob didn't have any food with him, but he did know they were giving food to people helping animals at the Celebration Station rescue center. The sheriff said thanks and told Bob he'd probably see him later that day.

Now Bob could restart his heart and continue on to the rescue center.

He finally pulled into Celebration Station and registered at the volunteer check-in station. Things were much different this trip. There were plenty of volunteers to help with the animal care, and it was more like normal workdays. Up at 7:00 a.m. and lights out at 10:00 p.m. Best Friends didn't really need any help with the animal care, but the new group, ARNO, could use help with special trapping projects. Bob didn't really care, trapping sounded good to him.

ARNO was working with the local officials to determine the highest priorities for animals at risk. There was an apartment complex off Causeway Boulevard that would be torn down in a few days. People had seen cats and maybe a couple of dogs hanging out there, could we rescue and relocate the animals before the demolition date?

Bob was ready to go, but first he had a small, furry problem he needed to resolve. What to do with Minew? Then Bob ran into Mike, one of the guys doing search and rescue work on his first two trips. This time Mike was in charge of the cat area. Bob explained his situation and Mike readily agreed to set up a cage for Minew to hang out in during the day. Bob already planned to let Minew hang out in the van with him at night. To make sure Minew didn't get lost in the hustle and bustle at the rescue center, Mike made up a big sign for the cage that read "Bob's Cat."

Now it was time to start rescuing the cats at the apartment complex. ARNO had a new volunteer with no trapping experience, but who was more than willing to help out. Would Bob be willing to take her out and show her the ropes? It sounded good to Bob; everybody had to start somewhere, and with two people they could cover more ground. Imagine Bob's surprise when the person turned out to be Carse, one of the cat caretakers from his second trip to Tylertown.

Bob and Carse headed out and found the apartment complex (not as easily done as pre-Hurricane Katrina; a lot of street signs and house numbers were still missing). They immediately spotted five cats right off the bat. Over the next few days they trapped, fixed and relocated all the cats living at the apartment complex. They never saw signs of any dogs, so the canines must have relocated themselves.

Things were moving along pretty well. Bob was trapping during the early and late hours and helping out with a few other things in between. Many of the volunteers had been there for several weeks and were getting bored with the day-to-day routine. The food wasn't bad, but not like you would get at home. That was where Norma, one of our volunteers, came through big time for the people at Celebration Station.

Bob lost a lot of weight during his first trip to New Orleans (after all, it was 100 plus degrees and he hardly had any time to stop and eat). Norma wanted to make sure that didn't happen again. For the second and third trips, Bob left home with dozens of cookies nicely packed in air-tight containers. Bob, being a reasonably nice guy (don't tell him I said that), shared Norma's cookies with the other rescuers. The cookies lasted about two seconds. It was like a mini-Hurricane had struck the rescue center. Everyone kept thanking Bob for the cookies. I guess you never knew what would make an impression on people.

That same night, a few of the rescuers were hosting an impromptu wine and cheese party for some of the rescuers that were heading back to their homes. The hits of the party were two dogs, Red and Canal Girl. Both had touching stories and both were very popular with the volunteers.

Red was a paralyzed Pit Bull brought in by his dad who could no longer provide adequate care for him. Red had no idea he had a problem. He would drag himself around the rescue center faster than anyone thought possible. He was so popular that the volunteers took turns sleeping with him in his pen. He even made it onto the *Anderson Cooper Show* during a parade.

Canal Girl was a Golden Lab type dog that had fallen into a canal. She couldn't find a place to pull herself out and was struggling to keep afloat. Then a group from Celebration Station came across her and knew they had to do something. Craig, a rescuer from New Jersey, jumped into the canal and helped the dog stay afloat until they could figure out a way to get her out of the canal. And, of course, now the rescuers also had to figure out how to get Craig out of the canal.

Finally, the dog and Craig were pulled to dry land. They became an item and Craig did the same thing Bob did when he fell for Sweetie in Tylertown; he was taking Canal Girl home with him.

Then it was time for Bob to head back to Maryland. This time he was bringing a record thirty-eight animals back with him. Most were cats and kittens, but he also had five Border Collie puppies and a German Shepard on his cargo manifest. This load would max the van out and then some. He borrowed a tape measure from one of the other volunteers and calculated and recalculated the space in the van. He could fit everything in if Minew rode in the passenger seat. Minew was cool with this so they had their plan.

Bob made the call to Phil and Hope, the couple that lived in the Knoxville area, and arranged for another night in their RV garage. This time Bob would make the trip alone. At least all of the animals appeared healthy and wouldn't require all the medical attention like the animals on the last trip.

As Bob prepared to leave in the morning, many of the volunteers showed up to help load all the supplies and animals and witness the mini miracle of fitting it all in the van. Bob wasn't all that sure he had it worked out perfectly and was relieved when they had everything and everyone packed into the van and the doors actually closed. It was time to bid farewell and start the long journey back to Maryland.

Bob made the trip with a quick overnight stop in Tennessee. He even got his macaroni and cheese again. He arrived at Rude Ranch amid a lot of unexpected fanfare. Most of our volunteers were present to give Bob a big cheer when he pulled up the driveway with his thirty-eight, four-footed passengers. Bob looked exhausted and relieved that we had so many people to help with the animals.

We quickly unloaded the kids and started the massive task of processing the new arrivals. They got quick medical exams and some even got baths. I think the puppies were by far the most popular of our new guests. In the matter of a couple of hours all the kids were settled in their new home and ready to take a nap. I think Bob was looking forward to doing the same thing. Another trip completed. Now we just had to find forever homes for the New Orleans rescues.

Volunteer Martha with Two of the Freshly Bathed Puppies

Bob was happy to return home from New Orleans, not because he missed me (although he said he did), but because we had a visitor from Boston dropping by Rude Ranch. It was Betsy, one of the volunteers Bob met during his second trip to New Orleans.

She was part of a different kind of Hurricane Katrina reunion story.

The normal Hurricane Katrina reunions had been families reunited with their pets lost during the Hurricane. Most were similar to the Bite Boy-Tyson family reunion. This one was the story of a volunteer who fell in love with a sweet orange tomcat she met at the Tylertown Animal Rescue Center.

Betsy first met Orange Boy when she pulled him out of his carrier and realized he needed a bath. He was very weak, but took the bath well and purred and hugged Betsy throughout the entire process. She spent as much time as possible with him over the next few days.

Then it was time for Orange Boy to make the trip to Maryland where he would be fostered by Rude Ranch. Bob was loading the van with the twenty cats and Sweetie the Cattle Dog. Everything was going well until he realized he was one carrier short. At first he started to panic, "Where did we lose the carrier?" He looked all over the cat room until it finally dawned on him; Betsy was saying good-bye to Orange Boy. She had fallen for this little guy and had no idea if she would ever see him again. She hoped to adopt him at some point, but knew things might not work out the way she planned.

During the three months we fostered this incredible cat, Betsy never failed to email and check on him. He was very sick and was recovering much slower than the rest of the cats. Then we discovered he had severe diabetes and began his new treatment.

Bob told Betsy about the diabetes right away, worried she would no longer be able to adopt him. Bob needn't have worried; Betsy was still determined to adopt him if he wasn't reunited with his family. Well that time had finally arrived; Betsy flew to Maryland, spent the night at Rude Ranch and made the return trip with her new feline friend.

Orange Boy settled in with Betsy and her family, especially with Rose, her adopted daughter from China. Orange Boy and Rose were best buddies and even slept under the covers together. This was truly a story of love at first sight.

Betsy with her New Buddy, Orange Boy
Photo courtesy of Betsy Wagner

Bob Visits the
Emergency Room

Bob and I have found that the older you get, the more aches and pains you get (or at least the more you feel them). It seemed once you hit forty, whatever warranty your body came with was up and there were no extensions. After that, it was down hill all the way.

Our problems started in January, 2006 when Bob was in New Orleans rescuing animals. He was trying to catch two cats in a condemned house and fell through the floor, jamming his spine in the process. The old saying: "it isn't the fall that hurts, but the landing at the end" certainly applied here. It hurt a little at the time, but he didn't think too much about it. We found out later the injury was a little more serious than he originally thought.

Several weeks after his return from New Orleans, Bob innocently leaned over to pick up Scruffy and felt an ominous pop. The pop turned out to be the sound of two disks rupturing. Before long, we were having loads of fun with doctors' appointments, referrals and the ultimate: getting an MRI.

The first attempt to get an MRI wasn't entirely successful. As you know by now, Bob wasn't a petite man, and he just didn't fit in the machine. It was like trying to stuff a two-inch square peg into a one-inch round hole. It just wasn't going to happen.

They finally pried Bob back out of the machine, and then it was time for another round of referrals to reschedule him for an open MRI. We found one about thirty miles away. Unfortunately, it was booked for the next three weeks. Bob didn't really mind the wait as long as the prescription pain killers and muscle relaxers held out.

Things rolled along smoothly until the day before Bob's MRI, when I slipped and fell down the stairs (I would normally try to blame Bob for this, but he was propped up on the couch hopped up on enough pain killers that he needed a bib to drink his diet coke. He was off the hook for this one).

Once again, the fall part wasn't too bad, however the landing, along with the twisted ankle and torn tendons did put a damper on the day. Bob graciously offered to share custody of his crutches with me. Between us we managed to hobble and crawl around the house enough to take care of the kids.

The day of the MRI dawned with me sucking down Aleve and Bob adjusting the crutches for my height rather than his. He headed off in the Rude Ranch van for the next adventure in diagnosing his back problem. Bob left on-time and didn't have to wait too long for the MRI. The open MRI went much better. It wasn't until he was walking out of the office and back to the van that things began to go downhill.

As Bob stepped off the curb, his knee popped and he and his MRI pictures ended up flat on the ground. Although Bob was sure the physicists of the world would appreciate his extensive gravitational testing, his new injury made it quite difficult to get up off the ground. His first step (so to speak) was to call the doctor's office he had just left. They told him they didn't handle emergencies; that's what 911 was for. After a few choice thoughts for the compassionate people at the doctor's office, he prepared to make his second call to me and realized the battery in his cell phone was going dead. He decided to save the phone battery and attempt to make it to the car on his own.

Using a car that just happened to be parked next to him, Bob managed to pull himself up off the ground (and he accomplished all of this without setting off the car alarm). Eventually, he hopped his way to the van and tried to figure out a solution to his next problem: how to get into the van and drive. He decided to risk the last of the cell phone battery and call home (as usual the charger for his cell phone was in the other car).

Bob's predicament gave me several options: on one hand, I already had plenty of pain killers for him (plus my handy back up, a cast iron frying pan) and plenty of ice packs; on the other hand, if I hobbled out to the car and drove down to get him, we would have a car stuck thirty miles away for an indefinite period of time. So I did what any wife in a dilemma like this does: I called Bob's mom.

Bob's mom arrived and we were off to rescue him. When we finally found him, he was propped up against the van looking like he wasn't having a lot of fun. I gave him a couple of the pain killers and loaded him in the back of his Mom's van. He didn't complain too much so I didn't have to break out the rolling pin or the frying pan. We made it back to the Ranch without much fanfare. Bob was happy with his pain killers and ice packs.

Now it was time for the standard fight over seeing a doctor. I wanted Bob to have his knee X-rayed and he didn't. I was basing my analysis on the fact that he couldn't put any weight on his knee or walk, and I still needed the crutches for my foot. He was basing his opinion on the fact that he didn't want to go to the doctor (such analytical thought from a math major). He changed his mind when I explained I would not be carrying him into the house (and I did still have the rolling pin and frying pan). He finally saw it my way and it was off to the emergency room.

We had enough experience with hospital emergency rooms to figure out how to get from the waiting room to an exam room as quickly as possible; massive bleeding, or a head injury and forgetting the president's name helped. It turned out broken bones also were a ticket to the fast track. Fortunately, I found a wheel chair to roll him into the treatment area. It was going well until the automatic door closed on his leg. While trying to get him away from the door, I also kind of banged his bad leg into the wall.

The X-rays didn't go any better; he slipped getting back into the wheel chair. Then the final straw came when we were waiting for the doctor out in the hallway. Bob had his leg propped up on a bench to take some of the pressure off his knee. That's when a paramedic pulled the wheel chair away from the bench without Bob's knowledge or consent. Bob's leg dropped straight down, bending at an angle it usually didn't bend. His voice also went up a couple of octaves. The paramedic did apologize, but Bob wasn't about to forgive him until the throbbing died down or I gave him more pain meds.

Soon we had a diagnosis: Bob had torn the meniscus in his knee and snapped off a few old bone spurs in the process. At least he got more pain killers. Now all we needed to figure out was how to share one set of crutches. Luckily, the knee doctor they referred him to was just down the hall from the spine doctor, and Bob wouldn't have far to travel between appointments.

Now Bob had his MRI results and the X-rays for his knee. We even managed to get back-to-back appointments with the two orthopedic specialists. Bob's sister Diane agreed to drive him to the appointments. I had other priorities that day, and to be perfectly honest, needed a break from driving Bob to doctors. He was developing a bad habit I was hoping he would break soon (no pun intended).

Diane and her daughter Gretchen took Bob to the doctor's office and were ushered to the spine specialist's office right away. As soon as the specialist walked into the exam room, she asked if Bob was the Bob Rude with Rude Ranch. It turned out we had helped her with some kittens a couple of years ago. It was another one of those small world experiences. She looked over the MRI results and confirmed that Bob did indeed have a problem with his back. Two ruptured disks. On the positive side, it wouldn't require surgery (at least not yet). Just stay off it for awhile and keep our fingers crossed that it wouldn't get worse.

Then it was time to hobble over to the knee doctor. This time it wasn't anyone we had helped out with kittens. The doctor still thought what we did was cool though. He had more good news for Bob, nothing major just some torn tendons that should heal on their own. Stay off it for at least four weeks and start physical therapy.

I knew I should have opted for the extended warranty when I married Bob, but I guess it was too late now.

Volunteer Adventures

While Bob and I were recovering from our assorted injuries, things were also happening for our volunteers, especially long time volunteer Lynn and her husband Ron. Lynn and Ron were long distance runners (Ron had competed in more than 100 marathons and triathlons). They were also avid animal lovers. This came into play during one of Ron's training runs when a small kitten ran out in front of him. It was only natural for him to bring it home. They decided to keep the kitten (after all it was really cute) and asked Rude Ranch if we could help with the vet work.

On the surface the procedure seemed easy enough: neuter the kitten, give him a rabies shot and send him on his way. Since this was such a simple straightforward surgery, Dr. Harrison had his newly-hired vet, Dr. Jantzen Strother, do the surgery. After all, what could go wrong?

It was Dr. Strother's first week on the job and his first "on his own" surgery. Still he wasn't nervous about the surgery; it was a neuter, about as easy as they come. The anesthesia went well, but then he ran into some trouble. The cat's testicles weren't where they were supposed to be. Being new to the job and wanting to make sure he wasn't missing anything, he checked with Dr. Roller, a more experienced vet at the clinic. She gave him basic instructions and moved on to her next appointment.

Dr. Strother still couldn't find the required parts. By now Dr. Harrison was wondering what was taking so long. It was a simple neuter surgery.

He decided to complete the surgery and hoped Dr. Strother would have better luck with his next one. Imagine Dr. Harrison's surprise when he went hunting for the kitten's testicles and found not only the missing testicles, but also body parts that only belonged to female kittens! The kitten was a hermaphrodite (possessing both male and female reproductive organs) and couldn't decide whether to be a boy or a girl.

Once the mystery was solved, Dr. Harrison completed the surgery and the kitten made a full recovery. Lynn and Ron named him Wingnut. Dr. Strother also survived his first surgery, narrowly avoiding a nervous breakdown. I don't think he really appreciated the experience, but at least he would never forget his first surgery.

Then Lynn called to tell us Wingnut was doing fine, and to let us know about a new TV show airing that night. The name of the show was *Dog Town*. We were especially interested in this new show as it starred several people Bob had worked with after Hurricane Katrina. The show was about the area at Best Friends known as Dog Town and would be based on stories of dogs they rescued. Sherry, the dog behaviorist, was to narrate the show and we heard rumors that Jeff, one of the guys who rescued Sweetie, would also be on the show.

All was going well until Jeff started talking about one of the dogs he rescued. As soon as Sweetie heard his voice, she sat straight up, bared her teeth and started growling at the TV. I guess she had a great memory and didn't appreciate the effort Jeff put into rescuing her. Sweetie may not have appreciated it, but Bob and I were happy he brought Sweetie into our lives.

Just as the show finished, we received a call from Hope, the volunteer Bob stayed with on his last two trips back from New Orleans. She and her husband had found a severely injured cat by their mail box that morning. Their vet said he had two crushed pelvic bones, his tail was severed at the spine, and he suffered from paralysis in his lower limbs. He would need a specialist if he was to have any chance of recovery. Not wanting to give up on this sweet cat, Hope called Rude Ranch hoping one of our vets could help him.

We agreed to take "Willie" and see what could be done for him. Hope and her husband Phil made the eight hour trip to Maryland. The next day we brought Willie to see Dr. Harrison. He agreed with the vet in Tennessee; Willie would need a specialist to repair his crushed bones, and even then, they may not heal properly.

We consulted with an orthopedic surgeon who, based on the X-rays, suggested the best course of action for Willie was cage rest. Keep him immobile for five weeks and see how everything healed up. So, for the next five weeks Willie lived in a special cage in the Rude Ranch living room. He had a lot of visitors wishing him well and giving him moral support.

When Willie's five weeks were over, we cautiously started physical therapy to help him regain mobility and strength in his legs. We were just hoping he would walk again. What happened over the next few months was nothing short of a miracle. Willie started walking and then running and jumping. You could hardly tell he had a limp. Even the vets couldn't believe he had recovered so well.

Although Willie was a wonderful guest, it was soon time for him to have a home of his own. He was adopted just before Christmas by the Beard family. His new family fell in love with him right away and told us he fit in wonderfully in their home. In honor of his Tennessee beginnings, his new name was "Jack Daniels."

Shortly after Willie found a home, we received a call from the Baltimore City Animal Control. Could we help with some tiny kittens that didn't have a mother? Bob made the trip and came back with four little orphaned kittens.

One of the kittens became known as "The Buffinator." She was mostly buff colored and we were watching the movie *The Terminator* when we named her. She was only eight days old and severely ill. She had pneumonia and distemper. Either disease could easily end her life; the two together made her survival seem almost impossible. Still, she was a tough little girl and we felt she deserved a chance.

We started her on aggressive medical treatments and around the clock supportive care. Ceasar, our resident canine kitten sitter, wouldn't leave the door to her room. We finally gave up and let him do what he did best, comfort and care for sick kittens. He would snuggle up with her and lick her face whenever she needed a little extra comfort.

Ceasar with the Buffinator and her Siblings

After four weeks of critical care, she started to respond to the treatments. In another two weeks she started eating on her own. She gradually gained strength and began to play like the little kitten she was. Her early illness probably contributed to her small stature. She never made it much past five pounds, but it didn't deter her from wrestling and playing with the big kids. She even developed her own fan club among the volunteers. Her biggest fan was our niece Gretchen. Every time she stopped by the house, she would have to spend some time with the Buffinator.

The Buffinator also discovered the joy of shredding paper, and would happily shred anything from paper towels to newspaper to important documents. She considered a career as a professional paper shredder with one of the top secret government agencies in our area, but decided life at Rude Ranch was just fine with her.

Now that the Buffinator was well on her way to becoming a healthy adult cat, we got a call from Denise, the volunteer who helped us with our newsletter. One of the feral cats she was moving to another colony tested positive for feline leukemia; did we have any room? We decided we could fit him in and made arrangements for his arrival.

Bubba arrived a few days later. Bob knew there was something wrong with him as soon as he saw him. He was very dehydrated and looked like he had lost a lot of blood from a wound on his lip. Bob started him on our critical care protocol and tried to find out what had happened to the little guy. We finally found out Bubba had been left in a trap without food or water for the four days he was at a vet clinic in Delaware. They had forgotten him in one of the rooms. He was in a humane trap and the wound on his lip came from trying to chew his way out of the trap.

We continued his critical care and he responded to the treatment. He would hug Bob and curl up in his arms. He may have been feral, but he really enjoyed his feeding sessions.

Bubba finally made a full recovery and was having a blast with the other kids in our leukemia room.

People could even check up on Bubba and his buddies now that we had web-cams installed in some of our rooms. The leukemia room had some of our youngest and most active cats and tended to get the most action from the web-cams.

The web-cams were part of our technology upgrade over the past year or so. Bob and Helen, two of our volunteers, decided to donate them to Rude Ranch as a Christmas gift. They even set them up for us. Along with the web-cams, we also expanded our existing web-site to include a presence on YouTube, Facebook, and MySpace. We tried to keep up with the changes in the "real world," but sometimes got bogged down with the day-to-day "fun" at the sanctuary. Fortunately, we had some technology-savvy volunteers who helped us keep pace.

Adventures in Plumbing

The maintenance side of running the sanctuary had been pretty trouble free for a while now. No major break downs, no doors falling off, no exploding toilets or sparks flying out of electrical outlets for several months. That only meant we were due for something soon.

It all started on a Sunday when a shelf in the linen closet collapsed. I was immediately told I made it collapse by putting too much weight on it. Silly me, I thought six bath towels on a shelf in the linen closet was reasonable. It might have had something to do with the fact that Tia and Billie Jo loved to sleep on the towels. That added about twenty-five pounds right there. Of course Bob never blamed the cats for anything. While Bob was fixing the linen closet, he decided to "check" the clothes closet, "just in case." The results were not good. Bob concluded the closet needed to be redone and I had too many clothes (of course I didn't agree).

The next day started with Bob making a trip to the hardware store for closet parts (ever noticed how guys always had to go to the hardware store)? Then he spent the better part of fifteen minutes taking everything out of the closet (and putting it on my side of the bed) so he could begin the "massive" repairs. The cats thought it was great, they had my nice, clean, cushy clothes to sleep on. By the time I arrived on the scene, I was again informed there were too many clothes (and shoes) and that was why Bob was spending the day repairing a closet instead of doing something productive. I kindly reminded him that his clothes were taking up more than the eighteen inches of closet space we agreed to when we got married, but that didn't seem to help his mood any. We eventually arrived at a compromise; my wedding dress and dry-clean-only clothes could be packed and stored in the garage. That was when things really went downhill.

When Bob tried to put the newly packed box in the garage loft, he took a hit of about five gallons of water, straight from the ceiling of the garage. That worsened his mood somewhat. When Bob returned to the bedroom and told me what happened, I could have responded in several ways: I could have laughed (he did look silly standing there soaking wet); I could have expressed sincere concern over his welfare or I could have run downstairs to survey the damage. My final choice of asking him if he was kidding didn't exactly generate a loving, heart-warming response. Asking if he had any idea where the water came from didn't help either.

We immediately changed our priorities from the closet repair to finding the source of the water. Bob tore the wet drywall down from the ceiling. That wasn't really helping his mood either; although he did seem to be getting some sort of sick pleasure out of tossing the wet drywall down to me (I thought it best not to mention he seemed a little too happy when I missed a piece and it hit me in the head). Sweetie kept trying to eat the drywall; it must be a New Orleans thing.

After a series of exercises that involved my running upstairs to turn various faucets on and off, and then running back downstairs to hear muffled updates, we finally found the leak. We had a cracked drain pipe coming from our shower. Since I was the last person to use the shower, the cracked pipe was also my fault. We knew this problem was way beyond our limited plumbing skills and called our fix-it guy, Joe. He seemed to genuinely enjoy the part where Bob took the water in the face. He said he couldn't work on it that day, but would be back in a couple of days to fix it.

Joe was good to his word and returned in two days. He even managed to plug all the leaks and Bob managed to patch all the holes in the drywall. We now had a fully-functioning shower and bathtub again. Ah, the simple pleasures of life.

Halloween Hyjinx

The fall season was soon upon us with all its assorted festivals and holidays. One fall holiday that usually didn't affect us too much was Halloween. Aside from the typical warnings about adopting out black or white cats, Halloween usually was just a normal day. We never had "Trick or Treaters" at our house. We lived in the middle of nowhere with one house on every five or more acres. Most kids figured they could score more treats per mile going to a housing development where they could walk from house to house. That particular Halloween was going to be a little different for us.

The day started off normally enough; we cleaned up the usual "presents" the Rude Cats left behind. Volunteers started arriving pretty much on schedule, and the assorted cleaning, scooping and feeding tasks were underway. At some point one of the volunteers came in and said she saw a kitten running across the yard. Knowing all our kids were accounted for, we went to investigate. Although we didn't find any kittens, we did find a dish of kitten food on the far corner of our property, leading us to believe there may have been some credence to the kitten sighting. Most likely someone left the kitten with a plate of food and took off, hoping the kitten would find its way to our door. A few minutes later, we confirmed the kitten sighting when Bruno found it and chased it up a tree.

We thought we had a few minutes to get a ladder and get the kitten out of the tree. After all, Bruno was doing a pretty good job of covering the ground underneath the tree and the kitten didn't show any interest in challenging him. The sound of five sets of footsteps approaching the tree must have terrified the kitten beyond any concerns about Bruno. It made an impressive twelve foot leap to the ground, slipped by Bruno and disappeared into the woods behind the house at full speed. If you have ever tried to find an eight week old kitten in two acres of woods, with thick undergrowth and plenty of fallen leaves, you can figure out how futile our search was. Admitting defeat, we set up a humane trap and went inside to finish our chores.

Later that day someone else stopped by to say they almost hit a kitten in the middle of the road. Figuring it had to be the kitten we had seen earlier; we looked again with no luck. By 5 p.m. we had another sighting, again in the road, but the kitten scampered back into the woods before anyone could get to it. We moved the trap to where the kitten seemed to be running into the woods and hoped for the best.

Thinking that most grocery stores wouldn't be busy on Halloween night, we headed out to do the week's shopping. As we were pulling out, we spotted the kitten in the road. We stopped and tried to coax it over to us. This time the kitten ran to the other side of the road, up a bank and scampered into a bunch of bushes about two seconds ahead of Bob. We later found out those bushes were composed mostly of poison ivy (Bob was itching for weeks).

We went to the grocery store and on the way back we nervously looked along the sides of the road for the kitten. We were almost to our driveway when we saw it, frozen in the headlights in the middle of the road. Not taking any chances, Bob stopped in the middle of the road, turned on the flashers and jumped out. The kitten again scampered off into the field across from us. This time we had help from the two young ladies who almost rear-ended us when we stopped.

We explained to a "Devil" and a "Kitty Cat" (we assumed they were dressed for a Halloween party) that we were trying to catch a kitten that kept running across the road. The girl/kitty felt she would be able to catch it, as she was already dressed as a cat (while there was some logic to her idea, I don't think the kitten was going to mistake this "slightly" inebriated young lady for its mother).

Both girls took off running, looking for the kitten. It was nice that they wanted to help, but what was really impressive was the way they were able to run through a field in three inch heels.

By now it was really dark (this was the country and we didn't have street lights). I moved the van from the middle of the road to the field across the street so I could shine the headlights out over the field. I left the keys in the van and took off to join the search for the kitten. Now we had Bob and me out in the field, and the "Devil" and "Kitty Cat" circling around the field. That was when one of our neighbors noticed our van in the field, lights on, keys in the ignition. He tried calling us at home, but we didn't answer. Thinking we were victims of some Halloween prank, he called the police.

Fortunately, the "Devil" and "Kitty Cat" were gone by the time the police arrived. Bob and I had fun explaining why we were running around a field at midnight on Halloween under the glare of the Rude Ranch van's headlights. No, we hadn't taken any drugs recently (by then the cop was thinking maybe we should be taking something). He wished us luck and went on his way.

Just after the officer left, we saw the kitten run across the road. This time Bob threw caution to the wind, lunged and grabbed a very tired and ticked-off kitten by the scruff. There was only one problem; this wasn't the same kitten we saw earlier. There was a second kitten (maybe more) out there somewhere.

We named the first kitten Wooly Bear and he was soon settled into one of our luxury two-room condos in the in-take room. Then the search started for the second kitten but to no avail. It wasn't until a couple of days later when the second kitten was spotted practically in our driveway. A stray cat living in our neighbor's yard had adopted the second kitten and had been caring for it the past few days. Eventually one of our volunteers lured the kitten over to her. Both kittens recovered from their Halloween hyjinx and were eventually adopted.

Just Another Day
at the Ranch

By now we had enough experience running the sanctuary to have the day-to-day routine down pat; still there were some days it just didn't seem like it was worth getting out of bed. This was one of those days.

The day started innocently enough; Bob got up early to sneak in a round of golf and didn't even wake me up. He called about an hour later to make sure I was awake before people showed up (I guess he didn't think the alarm clock would get the job done). Actually by that time, I was already awake and realized a couple of the dogs should have gone outside a bit earlier. The morning progressed with the somewhat normal incidents; the aquarium filter clogged and overflowed spilling water into the electrical outlet; Ziggy, one of our older cats, didn't cooperate with taking her meds, and Tommy sprayed the microwave. Then the two feral kittens scheduled to go to a barn in Ohio arrived. The kittens were vaccinated and deposited in a holding area (our bathroom). Things were getting better.

Around 10 a.m. it seemed things were going well enough to sneak in my exercise routine. I hadn't tied my shoes yet when there was a knock at the door. It was Jen, one of our volunteers. She and her husband George trapped a feral kitten and didn't know what to do with it. We settled on fixing the kitten and putting it back in its colony. However, the kitten needed a place to stay until it was fixed. We decided to put the kitten in one of our luxury two-room suites in the in-take room. Once the cage was ready, it was time to get the furry guest out of the trap and into the cage. That was when everyone, including the kitten, looked at me.

With much trepidation (after all, this was usually Bob's area of expertise), I reached into the long dark trap and managed to scruff the terrified kitten. I might have gotten the kitten all the way into the cage if another cat hadn't jumped into it first. That was when the kitten curled around my hand, rabbit kicked me with its hind legs, and bit the %*(&!!! out of my hand. I managed to keep a grip on the kitten, but I wouldn't call the way I deposited the kitten in the cage all that graceful. I managed to get the bleeding from the bite wounds stopped about a half-hour later.

With that adventure out of the way, I was still determined to get my exercise in that morning. I had just put on my shoes and started the DVD player, when there was another knock on the bedroom door: One of the two kittens headed for Ohio was missing. Of course it was the really, really shy one. It didn't seem possible, but the kitten had managed to completely disappear. Although we joked about it frequently, I generally didn't believe there was such a thing as the "Alien Feline Particle Beam Matter Antimatter Transportation Device." At that point I was starting to re-think the theory. After all, how many places could a twelve week old kitten hide in a 6 x 10 foot bathroom?

Then we saw an ominous thing; the vent cover for the air duct was pried off. Even more ominous was the little tip of a kitten tail that was sticking out of the air duct. In a moment of panic, I grabbed the tail tip, and ended up with a few black kitten hairs in my hand. The rest of the kitten (whose name was about to be changed from Jenny to &$*&^%^!) disappeared further into the duct work. That was when we decided to take an emergency training course on how the air ducts in the house were laid out.

We soon discovered the house had one main metal air duct traversing the house with flexible ducts splitting off it like spider legs. While this information would probably be helpful at some point in my life, we had absolutely no idea where the kitten was in the house.

This was the same kitten that had a one-way ticket to a barn 600 miles away in approximately two hours. That's when we pulled out all the stops. We removed the vent cover in the ceiling of the general population room downstairs. It was the closest vent to where the kitten went into the duct work and we were hoping she would still be close to that area. Our hope was she would wander down the closest path and jump to safety. Granted, a kitten falling out of the ceiling in the general population room might freak out the cats residing in that room, but in this place, we figured the cats had witnessed weirder stuff.

We put all kinds of tempting food outside the vent, hoping it would draw the kitten out. No luck. I guess she just wasn't a fan of Ohio.

Unfortunately, as the kittens' pick-up time neared, Jenny was no closer to putting in a return appearance. We figured we better start working on an alternate plan. We always had several cats looking for barn homes that were "circling the ranch" waiting to be waived in, so we made a couple of calls and said the first one here was headed to Ohio.

Shortly after that, Amber, one of our employees, arrived to take the kittens to her grandparents' farm in Ohio. Once she found out what was happening, she was a little concerned about the whole situation. She felt bad for the kitten lost in the duct work, but also knew her grandparents were expecting two cats. At least that problem was about to be remedied. Jill soon arrived with the back-up barn cat. Not to say this cat was mean, but when we tried to look at the cat, the whole carrier kind of growled. We decided we would just let this one hang out until Amber was ready to leave. No real need to examine the cat; it had been to the vet a few weeks ago. We packed the second cat up for the trip and breathed a sigh of relief. Amber soon left on her journey to Ohio with two ticked-off kitty cats.

A little later Bob rolled in and asked what I had been doing all day (at least he remembered to pick up a pizza on the way home). I really didn't want to give him the bad news, but I finally broke down and told him about the kitten in the duct work. Being a man, Bob was sure he could come up with a way to get the kitten out of the air vent. However, his way involved a lot of steps I wasn't too thrilled about, especially the part where he wanted to rip up the floors. Eventually we settled on baiting a humane trap with roasted chicken and hoping for the best. We wandered off to bed, hoping the kitten would be in the trap in the morning.

The next morning we nervously came downstairs to check the trap. Actually I came down nervously; Bob had that look of giddy anticipation of power tool use in his eyes. We cautiously opened the door (we figured with our luck the kitten would be sitting on top of the trap and head back towards the air vent). We were overjoyed to find a seriously ticked-off kitten sitting in the trap. We didn't waste any time, or take any chances; the kitten, trap and all, were quickly transported back to the foster home.

Although Bob was a little disappointed at not being able to rip the house apart, he settled for securing all the cat/kitten accessible air vents in the house. I was just hoping the cats weren't watching and taking notes for the next time.

Having narrowly survived this adventure with the kitten in the air vent, you would think we would never put another cat in that room again. However, Bob and I can be slow learners.

A few weeks after the kitten found the air vent, things were relatively quiet, except for Thanksgiving, Christmas, New Year's and all the ensuing stuff with the holidays. Just after the year started, we were approached by a neighbor who needed help with several feral cats in her yard. Thinking this would be "right up our alley" we met with her to discuss what she needed. The initial proposal didn't sound too bad, just help with the vet work, hold the cats long enough to recover and send them back. What could go wrong?

With the first cat, Cleopatra, things went pretty well; she was really scared, but could be handled without much trouble. Her stay in "the room" went well, although she did end up staying a few weeks longer than originally planned.

The next cat to arrive was Cleopatra's mom. Thinking the two cats would do well together and would comfort each other, we put the mom cat ("Momma Kitty") in the room with her daughter. We did start to question if the lady had the details right when Momma Kitty started nursing on the daughter. By the end of the day they were snuggled together in a comfortable bed, completely covering the air vent that had given us so many problems a few weeks ago.

The next morning we opened the door to check on "the girls" and saw the rear end of Momma Kitty disappearing into the air vent. At some point during the night, Momma Kitty and Cleopatra got tired of snuggling and started working on an escape plan. Either that or the other kitten that pulled the same stunt a few weeks ago left a note with an arrow pointing to the air duct. Momma Kitty was the first to go into the vent, with Cleopatra contemplating the prospect of joining her.

Remembering our previous experience with that particular problem, we decided not to panic and to give Momma Kitty time to realize the error of her ways and return to her comfy bed. After all, her spay appointment wasn't for another three days, so we figured she would get hungry by then and come back out.

Not wanting to take any chances on Momma Kitty missing her spay appointment, we moved Cleopatra to a cage and set up one of our humane traps with fresh roasted chicken and went to bed hoping for the best.

The next day rolled on with no sighting of Momma Kitty at all. At that point we were starting to get a little concerned, but managed to cover pretty well when Momma Kitty's person called to check on her. We just said she was settling "into the house" just fine. We were really hoping she would put in an appearance the next day. We reset the trap with tuna fish this time and went to bed hoping for good luck.

In the morning Bob went straight down to the bathroom, hoping like crazy there would be a cat in the trap (he was really stressing over having a cat in the duct work and really didn't get much sleep the last couple of nights). Bob was about as excited as a laid back Midwesterner can get when he found a rather annoyed Momma Kitty staring back at him from the trap.

Now we could get back to our original plans for Momma Kitty. Her spay went well and she was happy when Cleopatra rejoined her in the room. Hoping to prevent another tour of the air ducts, we developed a sophisticated system to secure the air vent: a blanket, two forty-five pound weights, and a full litter box placed right over the top of the air duct. True they wouldn't get any air flow, but at least they wouldn't get trapped in the duct work. Over the next few days Momma Kitty kept trying to move the contraption by wedging her body between the wall and the weights. We weren't sure if she was trying to get back into the air duct or was working on her abdominal muscles. Either way our security system seemed to be working and Bob could now sleep at night.

The Bunny Invasion!

Once again things at Rude Ranch were at a manageable level. We were getting better at controlling the flow of animals into and out of Rude Ranch, we had the beginnings of a low cost spay/neuter program, we had great vets, and some solid, reliable employees and volunteers. Fundraising was going pretty well too; at least we weren't dipping into our savings to keep things going anymore.

It was time to start planning our fall fundraising schedule. One of the main components of our effort was Boomer, the Miniature Pinscher. Boomer was very popular and the main reason we were invited to a lot of the federal agencies for their charity fairs. Our only problem was that Boomer, at the age of fourteen, was getting older. Although he loved the attention (and the hamburger he got afterwards), the hustle and bustle of the events were taking a lot out of him. We started to think about retiring Boomer from his fundraising duties or at least giving him a lighter schedule.

First we would need to "hire" a protégé to take over Boomer's duties. Bruno did well at events, but he was getting older too. Ceasar, still the most popular dog at Rude Ranch, was easily bored and would start looking for trouble. Scruffy barked at everyone and Sweetie, the Cattle Dog, was way too energetic to handle these events.

We were toying with the idea of bringing a new dog to Rude Ranch when we received a call from our friend Vivian. She was a retired

Greyhound rescuer, and one of our volunteers who transported cats and kittens to us from West Virginia. She had a friend that bred Miniature Pinschers and Dachshunds. Unfortunately, this person had suffered three strokes in the last year. His health was still questionable and he couldn't properly care for the animals anymore. Could we help him?

Being an animal sanctuary, we wouldn't normally take a dog from a breeder, but would find a needy soul from another rescue group. This was a little different situation; the breeder had way too many dogs as a result of his health problems and really needed assistance placing them. There was one Miniature Pinscher in particular that would be perfect for us and he wanted us to at least meet her. We figured what could it hurt and decided to go ahead and meet the little girl.

On a day filled with bad weather, traffic jams and more wrong turns than anyone thought possible, Bob met with the gentleman on his way back from an event at the CIA. It turned out the condition and number of dogs living at the house had been somewhat understated. There were about sixty of the little dogs living in a three bedroom house. They were receiving pretty good care under the circumstances, but there were definitely more dogs than the two guys at the house could handle. After suffering the strokes, he had fallen behind finding homes for the dogs, but the dogs continued to breed.

Bob met Blue Bunny, the dog that he picked for us. She seemed sedate and cute (we'd learn more about the whole sedate thing later). Bob decided to take the little girl along with one of the Dachshunds that someone had already agreed to adopt. Bob left with the plan to help this gentleman find homes for most of the dogs before he had any additional health problems.

Bunny had a few problems settling in at Rude Ranch. She was convinced she had to come inside the house to poop. She didn't just get in the trash; she burrowed in it, rolled in it and then ate it. She was afraid of everyone. We had to chase her around the house before we could take her for a walk. She acted like she had never been on a leash before. When she was on a leash, she wanted to be carried, a point she made very clear one day at a local pet supply store. When I didn't pick her up right away, she jumped up and grabbed onto my pants. That would have been fine if I hadn't been wearing sweat pants with loose elastic at the top. At least the guy behind me seemed to enjoy the show.

Bunny Hanging out at Rude Ranch

Bunny just never stopped moving. She stole food from people, cats, even the other dogs. At least she was an equal opportunity thief. She would climb shelves to get to the food. She even climbed to the top of a cat tree to get a plate of food. At one point we thought she was part mountain goat.

She barked constantly, at anything, even the other dogs. She even managed to out-bark Scruffy, our resident door bell. As aggravating as she was, she did have her good qualities. She got along great with the other dogs, not surprising considering her upbringing. She was also very protective of the cats. If one of the other dogs got too rough playing with one of the cats, she had no qualms about teaching the other dogs the error of their ways (it was kind of funny to see a twelve pound dog facing off with the 100 pound Bruno). Lastly and most importantly, she had the cutest way of cocking her head to the side whenever she did something she shouldn't have done. That must have been a built-in survival technique; how could you stay mad at something that looked so cute?

Bunny eventually settled down a little. Now she only barked when someone new showed up at Rude Ranch. She tried her paw at Frisbee too. She was great at running to where the Frisbee was going to land and then dodging out of the way. The part where she brought the Frisbee back still needed a lot of work. She usually picked it up and ran straight into the garage.

Her biggest challenge was learning to get out of the way when Sweetie came at her under a full head of steam. It took a couple of impressive crashes before she got the hang of that one. Now she just tucked and rolled when Sweetie came at her. We even took Bunny to a couple of charity events just to see how she liked them. While she was a little on the annoying side at Rude Ranch, she turned into this sweet, lovable dog at the charity events. She hopped from bed to bed at the Armed Forces Retirement Home and was a huge hit with all the residents. We thought she would work out great for these events after a few more pointers from the old pro Boomer.

Now that Bunny was settled in at Rude Ranch, Bob and I came to the conclusion we needed an occasional break from the daily routine of caring for the animals. After twelve years of the twenty-four hour a day, seven day a week schedule, we were starting to get a little burned out.

That's when we hired Casey to put the kids to bed occasionally. She had worked for us briefly in the past and had experience with medicating the kids. Now every Monday night and occasionally on Sundays, Bob and I could goof off for a little while. Usually we would just catch up on other projects, but at least it was a break from the normal routine.

Floating Down the River

Between the wildfires in California, record breaking tornadoes in the dust bowl and flooding in the Midwest, 2008 was the year for natural disasters. Some of the hardest hit areas were in Iowa where several rivers, including the Mississippi, Cedar and Iowa broke through levees and flooded vast areas of Minnesota, Iowa and Missouri.

On June 16th, Rude Ranch Animal Rescue was contacted by Brenda Shoss of Kinship Circle to help rescue animals from the massive flooding in the Midwest. Kinship Circle was a group that advocated animal rights, but also helped to coordinate volunteers for disaster situations. I checked Bob's schedule and, with a little shuffling, he could be free for the next ten days.

The Rude Ranch van was loaded with extra dog crates, catch poles, Kevlar gloves, medical equipment, dog and cat food, and we even packed a few things for Bob. Once the van was prepped and ready, Bob pulled out of the sanctuary at 4:30 in the morning, as always, in an attempt to beat the rush hour traffic in Washington D.C.

His initial destination was the Johnson County Fairgrounds in Iowa City, Iowa. This was the primary location to bring rescued animals in that part of Iowa. When Bob arrived he found the rescue center was well-staffed and not in great need of additional support. That happened a lot in disaster situations. The needs could change quickly from day-to-day.

Bob and several other volunteers were rerouted to the Lee County Fairgrounds in Donnellson, Iowa. The state officials were in the process of setting up a new rescue center to handle animals expected from additional flooding further down the Mississippi River. Bob and the other volunteers hopped in their cars and convoyed the seventy miles south to Lee County.

When they arrived at the fairgrounds, they found several employees from the Department of Agriculture (USDA) ready to set up the rescue center. Bob and the other volunteers were ready to help wherever they could. Just one problem, nobody from the USDA had ever set up a rescue center before. Barb, the lady who was to run the rescue center, had taken her husband in for chemotherapy and wouldn't be back for several hours.

Bob and the other volunteers had a quick meeting to determine if any of them had experience with setting up a rescue center. They all had some experience with responding to disasters, but none of them had ever set up a rescue center before. They decided Bob was the logical choice to oversee the development of the rescue center since he already ran an animal sanctuary. He would start setting up areas for the animals with the help of the USDA employees. The other volunteers Bob was working with, Debbie, Sandy, Kylie and Missy, would begin setting up the administrative and supply side of the rescue center.

Bob and everyone else were relieved when two trailers from Homeland Security arrived with a variety of animal supplies. FEMA even supplied a decontamination tent for the animals and humans that might be exposed to contaminated water. Thanks to the cooperation and hard work of everyone involved, the rescue center was up and ready to receive animals by 6 p.m. that night.

Then Bob met Barb, Laurie, and Joyce. They were volunteers who lived in the area and would be responsible for handling the day-to-day operation of the rescue center along with Katy, the disaster coordinator from the USDA. What a relief for Bob and the others, at least for a little while.

Shortly after things were settling down at the rescue center, Bob received a call from Brenda, "How do you feel about doing search and rescue of animals from a boat?" Bob told her he was rather large and depending on the size of the boat, he could end up rescuing animals from the bottom of the river. Brenda assured him that wouldn't be a problem. That night, Bob hooked up with Julius, the guy with the boat, to set up a base camp near Oakville, Iowa. The town had recently been evacuated, and now had the Iowa River running right through the middle of it. Most of the people in the town only had a few minutes warning to evacuate and didn't have time to round up all their animals.

Bob and Julius arrived on location, made it through security at the National Guard checkpoint and set up their base camp (a tent and a canopy in the middle of the road). Shortly after that the all important port-a-pottie was delivered. Now they were really living large.

For some reason their base camp was now very popular with the various emergency personnel in the area. Their first visitors were the National Guard troops manning the checkpoint into the area. Bob and Julius saw their military vehicle flying up the road at top speed. Something must be wrong. The National Guardsman hopped out of the vehicle and asked if he could use the bathroom. Julius calmly said, "Sure, just leave a quarter on the table when you're done." Maybe this was a new idea for a fundraiser. For the next few hours they had FEMA officials, the Army Corps of Engineers, and even a *Washington Post* reporter stop by for a visit. They left a sign on the port-a-pottie that read, "use at your own risk" while they went out to help rescue animals.

The next day Bob and Julius were joined by Dave, a rescuer from Alaska who was visiting his sister in Chicago, and Cheri, a rescuer from New Orleans who was a lawyer by trade (you never know when having a lawyer on your team could come in handy).

They met with Julie, Dan and Chuck of the Farm Sanctuary to discuss helping them rescue pigs stranded in the flood waters. Another group was now handling the rescue of the cats and dogs; so, they decided, what the heck, they would give the pig thing a try.

The entire team soon discovered rescuing pigs was a lot different than rescuing dogs or even cats. To start with, pigs weigh a lot more, and couldn't just be pulled onto dry land or into a boat. Also, pigs should be herded, not chased or pulled on a lead. Lastly, it was really hard to hold onto a pig that didn't want to be held!

Chuck and Dan worked up a plan that involved Bob, Dave and Cheri, some snow fencing, a couple of flat boards and a lot of luck. Two people would herd the pigs with the flat boards while the other three held the snow fencing at a point where the pigs were most likely to exit the woods. The pigs would enter the fencing, the three rescuers holding the fencing would quickly secure it into a makeshift corral and the pigs would be captured. Seemed like a heck of a plan. Too bad they didn't discuss this with the pigs.

Here was what actually happened: They managed to flush two pigs out of the woods and into the fencing. The three rescuers enclosed the fencing into a corral and had the pigs trapped. That was when they learned that pigs were very strong and yes, pigs could jump (maybe not as high as Michael Jordon, but much higher than either Dave or Bob were expecting). One managed to push under the fencing and escape, but they did have one secured, or at least it was still inside the makeshift corral. Now it was time to grab the pig. Bob managed to hook a catch pole around the pig's neck and then everyone dove on the pig. Chuck, Dan and Bob each grabbed a leg. After what seemed like ten minutes, but was probably only ten seconds, the pig calmed down and was "secured."

Now that they had the pig anchored down, it occurred to them that the trailer was a quarter of a mile away and the pig probably weighed at least 400 pounds. That was when Cheri and Dave volunteered to get one of the large pig crates from the back of the van. (We called them dog crates, but when in Rome…) They would load the pig in the crate and then carry/drag it to the trailer.

Things were going okay, the pig was relaxed, and Bob, Dan and Chuck were talking about other rescue stories, when a strong odor overcame Bob. He took a quick look at Dan and Chuck. No reaction from them. Bob was pretty sure he hadn't cut the cheese, so, it had to be one of the other two. Being polite, Bob didn't say anything. Then it happened again. Did I mention Bob had the back-end of the pig? The guys discovered that pigs can also have problems with gas. They all started laughing so hard they almost lost the pig. When Dave and Cheri came back with the crate, they thought the three of them had lost their minds. They finally stopped laughing long enough to explain their predicament. Dave and Cheri really didn't think it was all that funny. I guess you had to be there (or maybe the pig was putting out laughing gas).

Now they just had to load the pig into the carrier and drag it to the trailer. It turned out that dragging a crate with a 400 pound pig a quarter of a mile wasn't all that easy either. By the end of the day, there were five pigs in the trailer and a bunch of worn out rescuers.

Bob Relaxing with the Rescued Pigs
Photo Courtesy of Cheri Deatsch

Now it was back to the rescue center to help with the animal care. When Bob arrived, a new person was waiting to join the search and rescue team. It was Craig, the guy that rescued Canal Girl back at Celebration Station. As it turned out, almost everyone Bob was working with in Iowa had at one point been through either Tylertown or Celebration Station after Hurricane Katrina. Once they got to talking, a couple of people thought they recognized Bob, but they couldn't quite place him. Then one morning one of the ladies said she knew why she remembered Bob. You were the guy that brought the cookies to Celebration Station. It's amazing what people remembered. It had been more than two years and they still remembered the cookies.

The team made one more trip back to Oakville and determined the animals in town were no longer in danger from the flood waters. FEMA was beginning to let the citizens back into town to recover their belongings and hopefully to find their pets. Bob and his team worked with another group to set up feeding stations so the animals would have food until their people could return. A few of the local volunteers would maintain the feeding stations until it was determined what would happen to the town. There was talk by FEMA that the town might be condemned and the 400 plus citizens relocated.

Now that the emergency was over, it was time for Bob to head back to Rude Ranch. After all, I still had a lot of work for him to do here. He said good-bye to all the new friends he made during the trip, and packed up the Rude Ranch van.

Just before heading out, Barb showed up to say good-bye and thank Bob for all his help. She also gave him a parting gift, a stuffed toy cow that sang "Don't Worry, Be Happy" when you squeezed its hoof. I guess she remembered Bob was from Wisconsin and figured the cow was appropriate. Bob really appreciated the gesture and still has the cow proudly displayed in the Rude Ranch office. I still cringe whenever somebody squeezes the cow's hoof. At least it wasn't country music.

Barb had one other task for Bob on his way out of town. One of the cats rescued the night before was to be reunited with her family.

A call came in that morning from flood victims Tom and Jerri who were desperately trying to locate their twelve year old cat Tessa. They were part of the mandatory evacuation from Oakville the week before. They loaded their three dogs and pigeon into the van, but weren't able to catch Tessa before being forced to evacuate.

As soon as Tom described the cat to Laurie, she was positive they had her. Tessa had no tail and no teeth. A cat with that description arrived the night before. Laurie was positive about the no tail, but not about the no teeth. She found Bob and asked him if he could check the cat for teeth. Sure enough, when Bob opened her mouth, there was nothing but gums.

Bob loaded Tessa in the van and she was off to be reunited with her family. They were currently camping in a church parking lot in Wapello, Iowa where the Red Cross had set up a rescue center of the human variety. Bob met with Tessa's family in the church parking lot hoping it was the right cat (he was a little gun shy after the incident with Minew after Hurricane Katrina).

Bob shouldn't have worried, Tessa and her family were obviously very happy to see each other. Jerri told Bob she had celebrated her birthday the previous day, and seeing Tessa alive and well was the best birthday present she ever had! That was a great ending to a tough trip.

Little Tessa Reunited with her Parents, Tom and Jerri

Saying Good-Bye

Many people have experienced the loss of a beloved pet. We here at Rude Ranch were no exception. We followed the belief that all animals go over the Rainbow Bridge when they are no longer with us. For those of you who haven't heard of this concept, the following poem will give you a good understanding:

"Just this side of heaven is a place called Rainbow Bridge.

When an animal dies that has been especially close to someone here, that pet goes to Rainbow Bridge. There are meadows and hills for all of our special friends so they can run and play together. There is plenty of food, water and sunshine, and our friends are warm and comfortable.

All the animals who had been ill and old are restored to health and vigor. Those who were hurt or maimed are made whole and strong again, just as we remember them in our dreams of days and times gone by. The animals are happy and content, except for one small thing; they each miss someone very special to them, who had to be left behind.

They all run and play together, but the day comes when one suddenly stops and looks into the distance. His bright eyes are intent. His eager body quivers. Suddenly he begins to run from the group, flying over the green grass, his legs carrying him faster and faster.

You have been spotted, and when you and your special friend finally meet, you cling together in joyous reunion, never to be parted again. The happy kisses rain upon your face; your hands again caress the beloved head, and you look once more into the trusting eyes of your pet, so long gone from your life but never absent from your heart.

Then you cross Rainbow Bridge together....

Author unknown..."

Over the years, Bob and I felt blessed to have met so many incredible animals. While all have been special, a few forged an extraordinary bond with us. They also left an incredible void when it was their time to go over the Rainbow Bridge. We liked to think of them running and playing, free of any problems they had during their time with us.

Like most people, we wished all the animals could stay with us forever, but unfortunately that's not the way life works. As we humans feel our bodies' age over time, the aging process happens even faster for most of our animal friends. We were starting to see that in some of Rude Ranch's original residents.

Tia, the kitten Bob helped me adopt more than sixteen years ago was beginning to show the first signs of aging. Tia was the cat that helped plan our wedding, reluctantly gave up her half of the bed when Bob moved in, helped us start Rude Ranch and ruled over all the other cats, dogs and kittens that had since arrived.

At seventeen she was one of the oldest cats at the sanctuary. She was always very healthy until her early teens, when she was diagnosed with hyperthyroidism and kidney problems. As the years went by, we noticed she was having trouble jumping up on counters and desired the warm sunny spots for her naps. Then one day we found a lump on her thigh. That lump turned out to be two tumors, two cancers that had grown and wrapped around each other. Both cancers were considered aggressive. Without treatment she was given an outside chance of three months to live. The only option was to remove her leg at the hip. We decided to try the surgery and give her a chance to continue her life. Unfortunately, she did not survive the surgery. Although we missed her physical presence greatly, we knew her spirit was still with us, making sure all the other cats stayed in line.

Her Royal Highness, Tia

A few months later Bones, our nineteen year old mascot, was having some problems. The vets couldn't find anything specifically wrong with him. He was just getting old.

With his subtle meow and gentle disposition he was one of the more popular cats at Rude Ranch. He would patiently let children hold him and was a somewhat reluctant model for claw trimming demonstrations. Although he hated to travel himself, he frequently went up to frightened cats in carriers, trying to comfort them. He would even give mother cats a break, allowing their kittens to curl up and nap with him. He loved to chase the laser pointer, sometimes outrunning the younger cats.

Then one day he no longer wanted his favorite treats. His gums were getting pale and something was terribly wrong. Blood tests revealed his body had stopped producing red blood cells; essentially his organs were wearing out and shutting down. There was nothing we could do. There was no cure for old age.

We thought he had more time, but his body said otherwise. He climbed into my lap one morning and then started struggling for breath. We rushed him to the vet, but he died in my arms on the way. We will always remember his gentle spirit and unassuming acceptance of all creatures he met. Our mascot and one of our best friends was gone.

We also lost Queenie and Secretariat, two of the race track kittens. Of all the race track kittens, Queenie had been the sickest. She had the most eye damage and was completely blind. She and Bob were inseparable. If Bob was in a room, Queenie was outside the door. Throughout her short life Queenie acted as if her blindness was natural. She amazed people with her ability to navigate around people, furniture and even other animals. Not only could she navigate well on the floor, she also mastered climbing kitty condos, couches and even the climbing poles. Unfortunately, she and her brother, Secretariat, were born with severe heart defects that could not be repaired. By the time they reached their second year, their bodies grew too big for their damaged hearts to maintain and they died within a few weeks of each other. We will always remember their indomitable spirits and their joy of life. They were taken far too soon and will always be missed.

While we miss these friends and the many others that have crossed the Rainbow Bridge, we feel blessed to have known them all. We take comfort in thinking that in spirit they are healthy and whole, running and playing without regard to physical constraints.

To commemorate their lives and help us cope with their loss, we created a memorial garden for our lost friends. Each animal we must say good-bye to, has a hand-painted rock placed in the garden to remind us of how special they were. The garden consists of thousands of plants along peaceful paths winding through the woods behind the sanctuary. The entire garden is centered on a pond with a waterfall and stream. Our volunteers and visitors can enjoy nature while remembering their favorite friends too.

The Cat and Angel Statue at the
Entrance to the Memorial Garden

Santa Claws Brings CNN to Rude Ranch

By the fall of 2008, the Iowa rescues were over and becoming a distant memory, we completed most of our Combined Federal Campaign events for the year, and were approaching the holiday season. It was time to start promoting our annual Photos with Santa event now held each Christmas at Crunchie's Natural Pet Foods Store.

To ensure a big turn out for this event, I would beg, borrow and steal as much free publicity as possible. One of the publications that always promoted our cause was the *Bay Weekly* magazine, a local publication covering the Annapolis area. I sent them a picture of Bob as Santa with this cute little dog. I was hoping they would publish the picture along with the details of the event.

I thought I hit pay dirt a couple of weeks later when I had a message from the *Bay Weekly* editor. She was doing a story about local charities to be published around the holidays. Would we be interested in talking to a reporter about that? I just about set the phone line on fire calling her back. We did the interview and sent a few pictures related to the event and other happenings at Rude Ranch.

A few weeks later, several of our volunteers called all excited, "Did you see the picture of Bob in the *Bay Weekly.*" I just said "Umm, no, maybe I should pick up a copy." Sure enough, there was Santa Bob, not only on the front page, but the entire front page. Score! Even better, we were the first group mentioned in the charity article. That should really help get people out for the Photos with Santa event.

Just when I thought we had scored an incredible publicity opportunity, I got an even bigger shock. There was an email from Bethany Swain, a photo journalist with CNN. She was interested in interviewing us to do a holiday story to air on CNN. I read the message a bunch of times to make sure I wasn't imagining it. It appeared to be legit. What the heck, I gave her a call.

Bethany discovered Rude Ranch while waiting for her pizza at the local Ledo's restaurant, also the official pizza here at Rude Ranch. She was bored and started browsing through some of the literature on the counter. One of the items happened to be the *Bay Weekly* story on Rude Ranch. She read the article and thought we would be perfect for a story she was putting together for the holidays. She was looking for people who dedicated their lives to charitable endeavors. I guess she thought two people who quit their federal jobs to scoop litter boxes and rescue animals fit her profile.

We set up an appointment for her to visit and film the activities at Rude Ranch. We spent the next couple of weeks figuring out what to do for the filming (I gave up on trying to lose those thirty pounds and concentrated on the sanctuary). It was to be a holiday cheer kind of story, so we thought it would be a good idea to have a warm cozy holiday look. That meant digging out our Christmas decorations, dusting them off (pulling several cats out of the forbidden boxes) and hoping none of the Rude Cats took out the Christmas tree.

The day of filming started well with no major problems. Bethany arrived just as we finished the cleaning. We didn't know what to expect, but Bethany did a great job of putting us at ease. She told us to just "act natural" and go about our normal activities. We weren't sure acting natural would work, but went with it anyway.

She spent the next five hours filming Bob and me, the animals and even the adoption of one of our Hurricane Katrina cats (naturally it was a cat that hated going into a carrier, so she got a lot of footage of Bob and me chasing the cat around the room). The afternoon flew by and soon it was time for Bethany to leave. As she packed her equipment, she said the footage she took would be edited down to about two minutes and would air sometime around Christmas.

Then the day arrived. Bethany sent an email telling us when the piece would air. I had about twenty minutes to let people know. Fortunately, it was a Saturday and people were just starting to check their email. We anxiously stopped what we were doing and turned on CNN. The typical top stories of the day were on. Then just as they were heading to commercial, the news anchor said, "Up next, a touching holiday story about two people dedicating their lives to saving animals. Stay tuned for the story of Rude Ranch Animal Rescue."

We weren't even going to do our typical run to the bathroom or quick trip for a soda at that point. Soon the commercials were over and the news anchors were back. It was one of those surreal moments. There we were in our living room watching ourselves on TV. The story was well done and didn't make Bob or me look like morons. We were happy. Now we'd go back to our normal routine and could always say we had been on CNN.

The next day we received another email from Bethany; the story was a big hit and would be played a few more times. That was when we learned CNN replayed stories based on how many hits it got on their web-site. The more hits, the more frequently they aired the story. We were the number two story for that day. This continued throughout the holidays. We had people calling us from all over the country telling us they had seen Bob and me on CNN.

Dottie, a former volunteer, called from Long Island to let us know she heard Bob's voice coming from the TV while she was eating breakfast. "Wait a minute, I know those people." We received that type of call over and over for the next few days. It was an unusual feeling for two people who normally lived a pretty routine (boring) life.

As our story received more airtime on CNN, our web-site also received more traffic; a lot more traffic. At one point our web-site crashed. The inflow of people curious about Rude Ranch overloaded our normally low activity web-server. In three hours we had as many hits as we normally got in three months. We got more email than we could answer, all wishing us well. We were touched and overwhelmed by the response to the story.

Then we received calls from radio stations and TV production companies that saw our segment on CNN. They were interested in interviewing us and possibly doing a documentary or reality TV show about Rude Ranch. Who would believe the lives of two simple people would generate this much interest.

We still weren't sure where this would all end, but felt blessed to receive the support of so many people that believed in what we do... helping those who can't help themselves.

LaVergne, TN USA
24 September 2009
158841LV00003B/4/P